S0-BNF-959

What You Say Is What You Get

"What You Say Is What You Get"

Roger A. Golde

HAWTHORN BOOKS, INC.
PUBLISHERS/*New York*
A Howard & Wyndham Company

To my wife, Ellen

WHAT YOU SAY IS WHAT YOU GET

Library of Congress Catalog Card Number: 78–71080
ISBN: 0–8015–8530–9

1 2 3 4 5 6 7 8 9 10

Contents

Acknowledgments

I am grateful to Armajit Chopra and my wife, Ellen, for contributing many helpful comments and reactions. I owe a very special note of thanks to Judith Robbins and Robert Guttentag. Each of them reviewed the entire draft manuscript quite thoroughly. Their suggestions were both shrewd and substantial, and I have incorporated a great many of their insights. Their willingness to labor so long and attentively on my behalf was an act of friendship I deem rare and very precious.

What You Say Is What You Get

Introduction: What's Your Line?

> Men think with words, but seldom long about the words with which they think. . . . The more fully aware we are of the language forms we are using . . . the more of a say we have in what we have to say.
>
> —WENDELL JOHNSON

> Whatever man is, he becomes it by speaking.
>
> —JACQUES LACAN

As Ye Say, So Shall Ye Reap

Talk is something we all do, and we do it all the time. Just imagine that for a week you took a vow of complete silence. Think about the difficulties you would have in going about your daily job or conducting your family affairs. The basis for this book, however, is not just *that* you talk, but *how* you talk.

Through words you make friends, deal with family squabbles, and accomplish much of your career work. The positions you hold, the authority you are given, and the knowledge or skills you have give you power, but how effectively you use that power depends in large measure on how you talk. Much of what you want (or don't want) comes from your dealing with other people, and talking is your main mode of dealing with those other people.

This is not a book on semantics or linguistics. This book is not a "save the English language" treatise on better use of grammar

1

and vocabulary. It is not a book on how to be an exciting public speaker or how to be interviewed on television without making a fool of yourself. Nor is it about how to be charming at cocktail parties.

This book is about the important conversations you have every day with people at work, with your friends, and with your family. This book is about conversations in which you exchange information, solve problems, create ideas, make plans, reach decisions. The main thrust of this book is that what you say can help you get more of what you want: love and affection or self-realization; quarreling less with your kids or your spouse; motivating your subordinates or earning more money.

Talking gets things done, and the techniques in this book can help you

- express more accurately what you want
- motivate others to work more effectively
- be more in control of the conversations you have
- avoid needless arguments
- reduce the conflicts and tensions of dealing with daily problems

Talking influences what other people think of you and how they feel toward you, and the techniques in this book can increase

- the satisfaction others get from working or being with you
- the trust others have in you
- the closeness others feel toward you

There'll Be Some Changes Made
Will reading this book change some of your behavior? The odds are it will! You know that experts in the field of human behavior argue about whether you should change your attitudes and feelings first in order to change your behavior or whether you should try to change your behavior first and let that lead to the desired changes in attitudes and feelings. This book is squarely in the second camp—of working on behavior first. The unusual

premise behind the whole book is that *what you say is one of the easier* (and least publicized) *parts of your behavior to change.*

You probably already feel you should more often hand out praise, listen carefully, pin things down, be sympathetic, express your feelings. At least you realize you could benefit from doing these things, but often you simply don't know how to do these "good" things. Changing what you say isn't the whole answer, but it will certainly help. And changing what you say is something specific that you can do immediately.

Well, then, is this a book on how to be a "better" person or how to improve your self-image? Not really. True, there is a lot of evidence that the way we talk to others influences the way we talk to ourselves, and the way we talk to ourselves certainly influences how we think and feel. So perhaps using some of the techniques in this book will alter the way you feel about yourself, but that's just an extra bonus.

> *Thought is language internalized, and we think and feel as our particular language impels and allows us to do.*
> —GEORGE STEINER

What Can You Say?

This book deals with ways of understanding the other person, criticizing him, praising him, getting advice from him. Now, you have been doing these kinds of talking most of your life. But you probably haven't thought much about the way you say these things. High schools and colleges don't require (or even offer) a course like Talking 101. You've probably just picked up a few standard approaches for the various kinds of talking you do. For example, you may currently use some of these:

Verbal Approach	*Purpose*
"I hear you."	to show understanding
"Why are you feeling so depressed?"	to find out more about a friend's feelings

"That's a great idea, *but* it'll just cost too much."	to make a tactful criticism
"What do you think I ought to do on this?"	to get advice
"I can't do it, I have to spend time with the kids."	to say no
"Don't worry, it'll turn out all right."	to allay someone's anxiety

If you are like most people, you would have some difficulty coming up with even one or two different ways of getting across each of these thoughts. And that is precisely what this book is about: *helping you develop (or expand) your repertoire of verbal alternatives* —call them verbal formulas or recipes if you will. (And you will discover other alternatives for all the samples shown.) If you have alternatives, then you can select the one that will work best for a given situation, instead of always relying on the same verbal concoction or pat phrase. As psychologist Abraham Maslow has said, "If the only tool you have is a hammer, you tend to treat everything as if it were a nail." This book can help you carry more than just a hammer in your verbal bag of tools.

A Few Common Concerns

Isn't this whole approach of verbal formulas awfully manipulative? One is supposed to say something in a particular way to get the other person to respond as one would like. Sure, verbal formulas are manipulative—manipulative in the sense that one uses them to affect the person to whom one is talking. But isn't that what much of talking and communication is about? If you didn't think you could influence the person you are talking to, you wouldn't do much talking. It's not immoral to try to influence others, is it?

The term *manipulation* has a certain sinister quality about it. True, the techniques in this book can be used for devious purposes, as can any skill or piece of technology. It's up to the user.

This book, however, does not emphasize techniques for tricking or deceiving the other person; the orientation is not toward gamesmanship or one-upping someone else. The techniques aren't any more or less manipulative than the rest of what one says.

But aren't these verbal formulas still going to sound very artificial or insincere? Can one really put words in people's mouths? Doesn't one have to express things in one's own way?

No question. You should use the techniques you find most comfortable and adapt them to your own conversational style. But if you are going to try out something new, it is a lot easier if you have something specific and concrete to start with. This book typically provides several alternative wordings for each technique, precisely to make clear that no specific wording is sacrosanct.

The verbal formulas are not a set of hard-and-fast rules. Each technique is discussed in terms of how it works and the results it produces. The rest is up to you. True, some of the formulas are presented rather positively. But that has been consciously done to encourage you to try them out, not to imply that the formulas are right or better all the time for everyone.

But Where Do Verbal Formulas Come From?

Well, you see there is this huge laboratory filled with typewriters instead of test tubes. And hundreds of bespectacled men in white coats run around talking frantically to each other, testing out new verbal formulas.

Have no fear. Such a laboratory exists only in the fantasy of a Woody Allen movie. What does exist is a lot of relevant research and writing in a wide variety of fields, from philosophy to psychology, from semantics to salesmanship, from idea generating to interviewing. Some of the writings in these fields only hint at verbal techniques. In other cases, the verbal formulas lie buried in case histories or are quickly mentioned in the middle of more theoretical exhortations.

Of course, everyone also has a few pet techniques he or she has picked up along the way. And some of these are included too—

techniques picked up from friends and others with whom I've worked over the years. Some of the techniques are original, which just means I haven't heard other people use them or talk about them. It's always hard to trace the origins of anything in language —who first said what. Many of the verbal techniques have been developed or described by a number of different sources. What this book does is collect the techniques in one convenient place. Each technique, however, has been personally field-tested, that is, I have used all of the verbal approaches at one time or another to good effect.

Reading the Rest of the Book

The next two chapters cover several fundamental techniques: hearing and understanding the other person, and getting at specifics. Liberal use of these basic approaches is made in many of the subsequent chapters, which go on to cover such common types of talking as criticizing, crediting, getting advice, and saying no. Then chapters 7, 8, and 9 again deal with some general verbal approaches applicable to a variety of conversations. The final chapter provides an overview of all the various formulas and techniques, along with some suggestions for trying them out and incorporating them into your daily talk.

You can certainly read through the chapters in order, but you can also follow your own interests and read the chapters in some other order. Each chapter does make sense by itself. In any case, however, I would recommend not reading more than one chapter in a single sitting.

Some of the chapters ask you to state your opinion, recount an experience, or try out a technique with some of the sample phrases provided for you. Think of these activities as your chance to participate in what is certainly a very one-sided conversation. The chapters also include numerous quotations, which, if nothing else, provide a break from my own style. But also, "I quote others only the better to express myself" (Michel de Montaigne).

All in all, the book presents over eighty specific verbal formulas or suggestions. Obviously you aren't going to use all of them or probably even remember half of them. You are pretty sure, however, to find right away one or two techniques that appeal to you. Try them out and then later come back to the book and pick up a few more. Expanding your verbal repertoire is not an all-or-nothing matter. Whatever techniques you add and use make you that much better off. What you say is what you get!

1 The Most Important Thing

When another person discusses an issue with you, what is likely to be the most important thing that the *other person* wants *you* to do?

- ☐ to agree
- ☐ to solve his or her problem
- ☐ to offer helpful criticism
- ☐ to be sympathetic
- ☐ to act on what he or she says
- ☐ to respond frankly and openly
- ☐ none of the above

I have asked this question of a great many people, and the answers are pretty well split among the alternatives listed above. Now let me turn the question around: When you are discussing an issue with another person, what is likely to be the most important thing that *you* want the *other person* to do?

Have you got your answer in mind? The chances are your answer is something like one of these: You want the other person

- to listen attentively
- to really hear what you are saying
- to realize the position from which you are speaking
- to really try to understand what you are saying
- to signal understanding

At least these were the most common answers I received from the many people to whom I posed the question—the same people to whom I had also posed the first question. In other words, when we are the ones doing the talking, the most important thing we seem to want is *to be heard and to be understood*. And if that's what we want when we talk, the odds are pretty good that's what the other person wants when she is talking as well. Sure, the other person may want to get agreement or have her idea acted on or her problem solved. But she can probably tolerate not achieving any of those things. What she can't tolerate is not being heard and understood, having what she is saying literally not being attended to and perhaps not being comprehended. And this is relevant for almost every kind of important conversation, whether it involves criticizing, praising, advising, problem solving, idea generating, or whatever. When you stop to think of it, isn't it perfectly obvious, so obvious that it is often overlooked? If the other person isn't going to be heard and understood, why should she bother to talk at all!

> *I always talk to myself because I like*
> *to deal with a better class of people,*
> *but I found out that half the time*
> *they're not even listening and I'm*
> *talking to myself anyway. So why*
> *knock myself out?*
>
> —JACKIE MASON

What's Not So Obvious

That the other person wants to be heard and understood may now be obvious. What may not be so obvious is that the other person is not only talking to you but is at the same time talking to himself. He also wants to hear and understand himself. In fact the line between talking out loud and quietly thinking is not all that clear. B. F. Skinner in his book *Verbal Behavior* puts it this way:

> The range of verbal behavior is roughly suggested in descending order of energy, by shouting, loud talking, quiet talking, whispering, muttering "under one's

breath," subaudible speech with detectable muscular action, subaudible speech of unclear dimensions, and perhaps even the "unconscious thinking" sometimes inferred in instances of problem solving. There is no point at which it is profitable to draw a line distinguishing thinking from acting on this continuum. So far as we know, the events at the covert end have no special properties, observe no special laws, and can be credited with no special achievements.

So when the other person is talking, look at it as a form of thinking—thinking out loud, even if it sounds much more sure-footed or assertive than thinking. Realize that the other person needs a chance to hear and understand what he is saying, which may be one of the reasons he wants to talk in the first place.

> *How do I know*
> *what I think*
> *until I see*
> *what I say!*
>
> —ANONYMOUS

THE FIRST STEPS

Words are tricky. Even if the other person knows exactly what he wants to communicate, his words always deliver an incomplete picture, much as an artist's painting never fully captures the image he has in his head. Moreover, the same words mean different things to different people, because each person hears (and interprets) words on the basis of his own individual background and experience. A little placard in one manager's office put it this way:

> I know you believe you understand
> what you think I said
> but I am not sure you realize
> that what you heard
> is not what I meant.

On top of all this add the possibility that the other person may not really be sure of what he means, and you can see why the first step is to be skeptical about what you think you have heard and understood: *Don't assume that either you or the other person knows exactly what he is talking about.*

The obvious next steps are to get the other person to expand on what he is saying. Don't presume you know. Don't take a guess. *Just get the other person to say some more!*

> *We may never hope to understand*
> *fully what we say so long as we*
> *think we already do.*
> —WENDELL JOHNSON

The Power of Positive Silence

Maintaining an interested silence is one easy way to encourage the other person to say some more. If the other person hasn't really finished, your silence provides the opportunity for him to collect his thoughts and continue. In fact one of the greatest dangers to full understanding is *not waiting,* that is, breaking in to suggest a possible interpretation or, even worse, interrupting to lay out your own thoughts.

Even if the other person is more or less finished, the silence creates a pressure—pressure to break the silence. We are all unaccustomed to public silence. It makes us tense and uncomfortable. S. I. Hayakawa, the noted semanticist turned senator, notes that "prevention of silence is itself an important function of speech." If you aren't careful, though, the tension of the silence can get to you first, and *you* will end up breaking the silence instead of the other person.

So adopt an old interviewing trick and give yourself something to do during the silence:

Wipe something out of your eye.

Examine your pencil.

Even up the ash on your cigarette.

Count slowly from 1 to 10.

See if the other person doesn't continue on. Of course, it helps if you look attentive while you count or otherwise putter.

If you find the silent approach too awkward, try the closely related gambit of grunting one of these rather noncommittal signs of life:

"yeah"
  "unh hunh"
    "ummm"

I close my mouth in order to open my ears.

Encourage Expansion by Repeating the Last Few Words— the Last Few Words

Repeating the last few words of what the other person has just said helps remind him where he had gotten to and makes it natural for him to continue on. The repetition also suggests that you are listening (but it only does so if you are).

Be careful, though, because this gambit can make the other person a bit disturbed with the strange echo he keeps hearing if you overdo the repetition—if you overdo the repetition.

Asking for More

What could be more obvious? If you want the other person to say some more, just ask her for it. You may feel silly doing this when you feel you already understand what is being said—and of course if *you* understand, then the other person must certainly understand. But remember, the first step is to ignore your initial feeling of understanding and be a bit skeptical about it. Try one of these phrases:

"Go on."
  "Tell me some more."
    "Could you expand on that?"
      "I'd like to hear more on this."
        "I'm not sure I got that."
          "Could you repeat that?"
            "Would you say it another way?"
My own favorite phrase of this type is "How do you mean?"

The fact that this phrase doesn't make literal sense seems to add to its effectiveness, perhaps making it a cross between the noncommittal grunts and the phrases that explicitly ask for more.

General, Nondirective Questions

Almost any question you ask the other person about what he is saying will lead him to say some more. The particular question you ask, however, will also affect *what* the other person goes on to say. Now, when you aren't too sure of what the other person is really saying, you may be best off asking a question that isn't too focused, that leaves plenty of room for the other person to go on talking about what *he* wants to talk about. These kinds of questions can be called general or nondirective. (Chapter 9 goes into more detail about the difference between various types of questions.)

Certainly positive silence and explicit requests for more are very general, nondirective types of response. But there are also some questions that won't bias very much what the other person goes on to say. For example:

"How do you feel about it?"

"What did you do?"

"What do you have in mind?"

"What are you trying to get at?"

"What is your reaction?"

"What happened then?"

Think of this whole approach in terms of your wandering around in a very dimly lit cavern (the other person's head). You don't really know what to look for and you can't see very well what is there anyway. So you're better off relying on your guide (the other person) who is somewhat familiar with the cavern and has some idea of what he might like to show you. You can't tell your guide specifically where to take you. But you can ask him to turn his lantern on a bit brighter and point it in the direction he would like to go (which you do via a general, nondirective question).

Later on in the discussion, once you have a sense of where the other person is going, you may well want to ask some very detailed questions to clarify what is being said. This approach is covered in the next chapter.

Do all these techniques for getting the other person to say more sound a bit psychiatric? Perhaps they do, but then aren't psychiatrists expert at getting other people to talk? Come to think of it, maybe if people used these techniques more often, there might be fewer people seeing psychiatrists.

PROVING YOU UNDERSTAND

Okay, so you're listening like crazy, you've disregarded your first impulse that says you have heard and understood, you've asked for more. Then you feel for the second or third time that you have pretty well heard and understood. Now what do you do? Many people say something like one of these:

"I hear you."	"I can relate to that."
"I got it."	"Good point!"
"I know just how you feel."	"I understand what you're saying."

But every single one of these phrases merely *asserts* your understanding. Not a one of them proves it, and that's the problem. A school principal put it this way: "My biggest concern when I talk with one of my administrators or teachers is that they don't really understand. Oh, they assure me they do, but somehow I just don't feel they do, and I don't know what to do about it." In other words, being on the receiving end of one of these phrases doesn't really satisfy the other person's need to feel truly heard and understood.

Paraphrase Your Way to Better Understanding
Sounds like the title of a best seller, yes? But the technique of paraphrasing is really a highly effective way to prove your understanding.

Paraphrasing—sometimes called restating or reflecting —has two equally important elements:	par·a·phrase (par'ə fraz'): to say in other words; a rewording of the meaning expressed in something spoken or written.

1. to rephrase back what you think was said
2. to get agreement to your rephrasing

If you do just the first part—the rephrasing back—then you have proved merely that you are trying to understand. It is only when you get agreement that your rephrasing is accurate that you have truly proved your understanding. Here is a little situation that involves the use of paraphrase:

JULIE—a long-time employee in the accounting department of the Frobisch Company

KELLY—a friend of Julie's who works in the production department of the same firm

Julie is talking with Kelly over lunch in the company cafeteria. Part of their conversation goes like this:

JULIE: . . . and so, you see, I'm worried that if I take off two weeks next month for vacation, the boss may be really upset because of the work he'll have to do with my people.

KELLY: It sounds as if what you're really worried about is that you think your boss wants you around next month. Is that it?

JULIE: Not exactly. I mean my boss says he'd be willing to have me take off. I'm just worried that some of the problems that come up may be tricky, and he won't know how to handle them.

KELLY: So, if I understand you, the issue is that you feel your boss might not be able to handle some of the tricky problems that could come up. Right?

JULIE: Well, that's sort of it, but, you see, the new man in my group is just not used to dealing with the boss, and they don't know each other very well. But the guy is very competent.

KELLY: Okay, what you're really saying is that your new man could probably handle the problems, but he might not be able to handle your boss effectively, and you feel responsible for the problems that might occur because of this. Yes?

JULIE: Yeah, I think that's pretty much it.

You may think this example is untypical because it took Kelly three tries to get Julie to agree with his paraphrase. Yet I ran an actual on-the-job experiment with approximately twenty pairs of bosses and subordinates. The average number of paraphrases necessary to reach agreement was over four, and in a number of cases six or more tries were necessary. It is truly surprising (and frustrating) to discover how much effort it takes to get agreement to a paraphrase—which only underlines how far from true understanding we are in most conversations.

> A story made the rounds some time ago about an American tenor singing his first concert in Italy. The tenor concluded his recital with a traditional Italian selection. The audience went wild. The singer repeated the final selection as an encore. Again more shouts and screams from the listeners. Once more he sang the song.
>
> The cycle continued until finally the tenor held up his hands saying, "I'm overcome by your response, but it's been a long recital. I'd like to repeat the song again, but I am very tired. I hope you understand."
>
> From the back of the concert hall a shrill voice yelled out, "You'll sing it again—and again—and again—until you get it right!"

Sometimes you can reduce the number of paraphrases needed to gain agreement by using more of the other person's words than your own. Of course, if you use all the other person's words, then *you* may not be sure you are interpreting them correctly. So just pick up some of the other's key words verbatim, but string them together a little differently (to avoid literal parroting). By the way, if you find what the other person has said too long to paraphrase, just ask her to summarize what she has said and then try to paraphrase the summary.

No matter what you do, however, be prepared for some difficulty in gaining agreement to your restatement. You see, even playing back an exact tape recording of what someone says is no guarantee that it will be accepted by that person as what was meant. For instance, look back to the Julie-Kelly conversation on page 15 and note that Kelly's second paraphrase almost literally repeated Julie's exact words, yet he still didn't get agreement. In fact, Julie went on to add another piece of information about the "new man" in the group. Crazy, isn't it? Well, not really, if you remember that Julie may be finding out what she really means at the same time Kelly is.

Some Typical Reactions

Here are some of the reactions expressed by the people who participated in the on-the-job paraphrase experiment mentioned earlier:

"By the time I really understood what he was saying, I realized my initial position had changed."

"I got damn frustrated, but more important information came out than I think would have otherwise."

"I felt relieved that we seemed to be working on a difficult problem without irritating each other the way we sometimes do."

"I felt a great responsibility to listen and concentrate—more than usual. I felt more aware of her reactions to what I was saying."

"We were able to focus in on what was at first a difference of opinion. It really turned out to be both of us saying the same thing in different ways."

What's in a Paraphrase?

There is no rigid formula for constructing your paraphrases. Your restatements can range from relatively literal repetition of the other person's words to using mostly your own words. You may decide to condense or summarize a little or even add a cautious bit of interpretation. Your paraphrase can include just the factual content of what you hear, or you can also reflect some of the feelings and attitudes you believe are being expressed (as Kelly did in his third paraphrase back in the sample conversation on page 16).

While the ingredients of your paraphrase may vary from situation to situation, the introduction should follow a fairly standard approach. The key is to state your paraphrase as a *form of question*, that is, you are *checking out* your understanding, not asserting it. A number of introductory phrases can serve this purpose. Several were used in the Julie-Kelly conversation, and they are shown below in parentheses along with several additional phrases:

("It sounds as if. . . . Is that it?")

("So, if I understand you. . . . Right?")

("What you're really saying is. . . . Yes?")

"Are you feeling that . . . ?"

"Is what you mean . . . ?"

"Is what I'm hearing that . . . ?"

"Let me see if I've got it. . . ."

Using Paraphrase

At the end of this section there is a summary chart showing the various steps and techniques presented in this chapter. This special process for hearing and understanding the other person is often required for several reasons:

1. Most of us have developed the habit of tuning in and out frequently as someone else talks. So we can miss an important part of what is being said.
2. Our mind speed greatly exceeds speech speed. So we may jump ahead to what we think the other person is going to say, or start developing our own reply.

3. We can easily mishear or misinterpret what the other person is saying because *(a)* words can be ambiguous and *(b)* words mean different things to different people.
4. The other person may not be sure of what he is saying.

You may feel a bit awkward when first trying out this special process in an actual situation. But the nice thing about the process is that you can follow it without needing a lot of practice. You see, the other person will tell you how to fix what you are doing once he sees that you are really trying to understand him. First, the very effort of trying to hear and understand demonstrates to the other person that you care about what he is saying. Second, that other person has an important stake in helping you perfect your understanding. In addition, the paraphrase technique makes it easy for the other person to help you work toward a better understanding. So if you end up having to ask a few extra questions or you require a few extra tries at paraphrasing, the other person won't really mind at all.

By the way, once you are a bit familiar with the process, you may want to turn the process around and use it to be sure the other person is hearing and understanding you. This reverse process would flow in a way quite parallel to that shown on the summary chart:

Disregard the other person's first impulse
that indicates he has heard and understood.

Provide some more.

Ask the other person to restate what he
thinks you have said.

Agree (or not) that the other person's
paraphrase captures what you mean.

Now, this whole special process for hearing and understanding may seem relatively cumbersome or complicated. Do you always need to use it? Certainly not.

- Sometimes real understanding just isn't that crucial.
- Sometimes the other person may not really want to clarify what he is saying.
- Sometimes vagueness is necessary to reach a useful compromise or consensus.
- Sometimes there is no chance to check out understanding, for example, if someone yells "Fire!" you probably shouldn't ask for more or respond with, "As I understand it, what you're saying is that you think the house is on fire, right?"

Unfortunately, you probably should use the special process for hearing and understanding more often than you might think or would like. Using the process can seem like the long way around, but more often than not it saves time in the long run. Much of the time we don't really understand each other as well as we need to, and that lack of understanding ends up costing us money or time and even friendship or love.

The special process is particularly valuable when

- the topic under discussion is important
- action is to be taken based on the conversation
- you are inclined to ignore, reject, or disagree strongly with what the other person is saying
- you feel angry about what the other person is saying
- the other person keeps repeating or insisting on what he is saying.

Truly hearing and understanding the other person is "the most important thing." It is so fundamental that you will find it referred to over and over in many of the chapters that follow, so get used to paraphrasing—again and again—until (like the American tenor) you get it right!

SUMMARY CHART
STEPS IN THE PROCESS
OF HEARING AND UNDERSTANDING

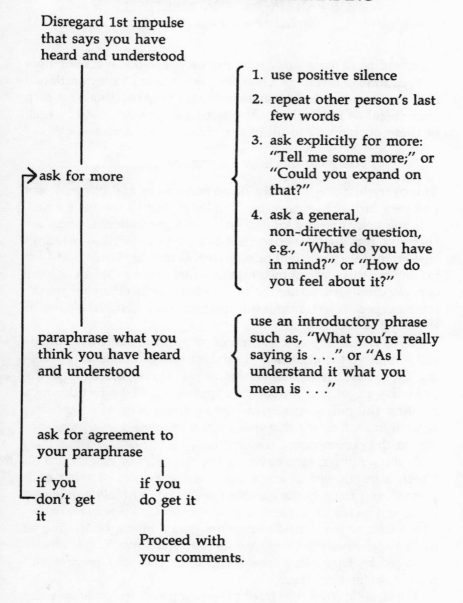

Disregard 1st impulse
that says you have
heard and understood

→ ask for more

1. use positive silence

2. repeat other person's last
few words

3. ask explicitly for more:
"Tell me some more;" or
"Could you expand on
that?"

4. ask a general,
non-directive question,
e.g., "What do you have
in mind?" or "How do
you feel about it?"

paraphrase what you
think you have heard
and understood

use an introductory phrase
such as, "What you're really
saying is . . ." or "As I
understand it what you
mean is . . ."

ask for agreement to
your paraphrase

if you
don't get
it

if you
do get it

Proceed with
your comments.

BONUS SECTION—A SPECIAL USE
OF PARAPHRASE IN MEETINGS
The Technique of Public Writing

According to some surveys, managers spend 50 percent or more of their time in meetings. Over the past decade I have questioned well over two hundred businessmen about the meetings in which they spend so much time. One particular question I asked each of these people was to fill in the blank in this statement:

I feel most meetings I go to are _____.

The overwhelming majority of responses are highly consistent and very biting: Meetings are "too long" and "a waste of time."

If you belong to any kind of group or organization, chances are that you, too, spend a good deal of time in meetings—meetings that are not very efficient or effective. (I should clarify that I am talking primarily about meetings in which some problem or issue is being discussed, rather than informational meetings where the main purpose is to transmit information or exchange the news of the day.)

Public writing is a special form of paraphrase that will dramatically improve the quality and productivity of almost any meeting. Of course, the regular version of paraphrase, discussed in the preceding pages, can certainly be applied to good effect during a meeting. But public writing involves a *written* form of paraphrase, written in such a way that it is *visible to all members of the group,* not just to the person doing the writing.

Public writing means having a big easel pad or blackboard on which a public writer notes down a paraphrase of what each person says. Usually the paraphrase will be in highly condensed form, and it is desirable to *pick up the exact key words used by the speaker.* The public writer can save time by paraphrasing orally first to make sure he has got it right before jotting it down. Time can also be saved by *using abbreviations freely,* since everyone present will readily understand them.

If the public writer has trouble knowing how to condense what someone has said, all he has to do is ask the participant to help him with the summary. If an easel pad is used, then the public writer may want to tear off each page when it is full and post it up in the room to keep it accessible and in full view.

Public writing does not mean recording only what the group decides on or only what everyone is in agreement about. The public writer should keep track of almost everything that is said, because it is important to the person who said it (regardless of whether anyone else thinks it is important or whether anyone else agrees with it).

The public writer need not be particularly experienced. He is a recorder, not a controller. Once the group members get the idea that someone is trying to keep track of what is being said, they will take over; they will tell the public writer how to fix what he has written if it doesn't correctly reflect what they meant.

It's usually better if the public writer is not the leader of the meeting. So if you are the leader, ask someone else to keep track of things on an easel pad or blackboard. (You probably will have to remind the public writer from time to time to jot something down, and not wait for agreement or consensus.) If you aren't the group leader, then just ask the leader whether he minds if you keep track of things by jotting them down in front of the group.

Here's why public writing works so well. Participants in meetings have the same fundamental need as when they talk to each other individually. People in meetings desire agreement, action, or whatever, but they can tolerate not getting those things. What they cannot tolerate is a failure to be heard and understood— otherwise why bother coming to the meeting? When someone in a meeting feels he isn't being heard or understood, he will tend to ramble on or repeat the same thing over and over at various intervals, or he may withdraw his energy from the meeting altogether and sullenly wait out the session. None of these reactions leads to a very productive meeting.

What public writing does is to *prove* to each person that he is being heard and understood, at least by the person doing the public writing. What in fact happens is that the very process of the public writing causes many other people in the group also to hear and focus on what is being said.

The other great value of public writing is that the notes are up in front of everyone so that they can be easily reread or referred to by each individual whenever he chooses. This helps a great deal because our brains have a very limited capacity to process or work on a number of ideas at the same time. Having the notes available for reference encourages the group members to build on things said previously, because the previous thoughts are up there—to be used. As a result, public writing greatly reduces the amount of rambling that occurs; the participants tend to keep on some common track instead of wandering off on their own individual avenues of thought.

Now, don't confuse a public writer with a secretary keeping minutes of the meeting on a small notepad, then typing up the notes and circulating them after the meeting. Keeping minutes can serve a useful purpose, but it is not the same thing as public writing. Keeping minutes does not prove to a participant in the meeting that he is being heard and understood *at the time he is talking.* And minutes don't keep the ideas in view for everyone's reference.

Oh, by the way, you don't even have to wait for a full-scale meeting to try out public writing; it works in one-to-one conversations as well. For instance, a number of successful salesmen use this technique all the time with individual customers. These salesmen find the customer is flattered, reassured, and pleased by their public note taking. The customer sees it as an indication that the salesman cares about understanding and remembering what the customer is saying.

In any case, try public writing in some of your meetings. You'll be pleased with the results, and who knows, you may get a memorial easel named after you.

2 Getting Down to Specifics

There's an old story about an elegant Park Avenue matron who lost her dog and placed an ad promising a handsome reward for his return. The ad described the dog as brown, male, and very shaggy. A tramp resting on a Central Park bench was idly scanning the classified section of a left-behind newspaper. As he chanced upon the matron's lost dog ad, up sidled a very, very shaggy, brown male stray dog. There was no question in the tramp's mind; this was the shaggiest dog he had ever seen. He grabbed the dog in his arms and raced off to claim the reward. In her vestibule the matron took one look at the dog and the tramp, arched her eyebrows, and said rather icily, "Oh, good heavens, he wasn't that shaggy!"

A To-the-Point Sales Pitch

- Do you find what other people say is sometimes fuzzy or confusing?
- Do you ever do something for somebody and then discover that it wasn't what was wanted at all?
- When you want advice or information from an expert or a friend, do you have trouble getting anything useful?
- When something goes wrong, do you have difficulty finding out what really happened?

25

If you answered yes to any of these questions, then you need our special handbook. After talking with hundreds of people from all walks of life, we think we've uncovered the secret key for dealing with these problems and many more. The magic approach is getting down to specifics. Now you can learn the special, most effective ways to do this—techniques used by highly successful courtroom lawyers, top salesmen, and fast-track executives. Apply the techniques every day to your problems at home and on the job. Use them to have a more meaningful relationship with your loved ones. Use them to get more out of your employees or to understand your boss better. You'll be really clear about what other people are saying. You'll avoid unnecessary confusion, improve your understanding of others, and cut down on needless mistakes.

And where action is needed, well, the specifics really pay off, because actions have to be specific. You can't buy "any" car or borrow "some" money. An appointment for "sometime" is not much of an appointment. As Aunt Tillie always said, "Anytime is no time" and "Anything is nothing."

But there's more. You can use these very same techniques on yourself to make your criticism more acceptable to others. When you give instructions, others will really know what you want. When you praise other people with specifics, they'll walk out the door three feet off the floor. Stop boring the people you talk to and really turn them on instead. Make your speeches more meaningful and your everyday conversation more exciting and interesting.

We're really proud that we are now able to offer this marvelous handbook to you. This exclusive edition will not be reprinted once the current supply is exhausted. Orders will be filled on a first-come, first-served basis. So act promptly and get the jump on your neighbors and fellow workers. The modest cost is fully refundable within ten days if you don't find something you can use immediately. Simply fill out the enclosed coupon and attach your check or money order for . . .

Okay, okay, so this other special handbook never really existed. But are the claims of the promotion piece exaggerated? Not really, because getting down to specifics really does pay off in a great variety of situations. But before delving into the specific techniques, consider the question of why any special techniques are needed at all. Why aren't the specifics naturally there in our conversations when we need them?

> *The wheels of diplomacy often turn*
> *on the grease of ambiguity.*
>   —ANONYMOUS

The Habit of Generality
"I'm feeling a bit under the weather."

"You know, Joe's report seemed pretty good."

"My line of work is sales."

"We've just got to improve our communications with each other."

"I somehow don't seem to have enough time."

Our daily conversation abounds with generalities. We even talk about the need for specifics in a general way: "Let's get down to the nitty-gritty."

And there are good reasons for being general. Social generalities (or pleasantries) can allow two people to get acquainted slowly without unduly threatening one another's sense of privacy; or they can serve as convenient ways to start off any kind of conversation.

But the vagueness or ambiguity of generalities is also helpful in more serious situations. Vagueness may make it easier to adapt to changing conditions. . . . Vagueness may make it possible to work towards many goals that can only be attained by indirection. . . . Above all, vagueness is an essential part of all agreements resulting from compromise. When a dispute is resolved some degree of ambiguity enters into the terms of settlement. . . . Certain anticipated situations are always referred to in terms that mean different things to different people, and are valuable because of, not despite, this characteristic.*

*Bertram Gross, *The Managing of Organizations* (New York: Free Press, 1964).

Many sociologists and psychologists believe that one of man's unique (or at least most useful) traits is his ability to generalize. Generalities are extraordinarily convenient. They spare us the time of reconstructing things over and over again from the specifics. Generalities reduce the clutter of trying to carry around all the specific instances on the tip of our tongues.

The value of generalizing is most exquisitely conveyed by an example of one who cannot generalize. "Funes the Memorius" is a short story by the Argentinian author Jorge Luis Borges. Funes is one day thrown by a horse, and when he recovers consciousness, he finds he has the ability to observe every detail and forget nothing.

> He knew by heart the forms of the southern clouds at dawn on the 30th of April, 1882, and could compare them in his memory with the mottled streaks on a book in a Spanish binding he had only seen once. . . . These memories were not simple ones; each visual image was linked to muscular sensations, thermal sensations, etc. . . . In fact Funes remembered not only every leaf of every tree of every wood, but also every one of the times he had perceived or imagined it. . . . Not only was it difficult for him to comprehend that the generic symbol *dog* embraces so many unlike individuals of diverse size and form; it bothered him that the dog at three fourteen (seen from the side) should have the same name as the dog at three fifteen (seen from the front). His own face in the mirror, his own hands, surprised him every time he saw them.

Borges's portrait of Funes is at heart full of pathos because, as Borges says, Funes could not "forget differences, generalize, or make abstractions." Even sleep was very difficult for Funes.

The Uniqueness of Our Thoughts and Words
Because generalities are often convenient and efficient, we tend to forget the uniqueness of our individual thoughts and the

words we use to express them. We don't fully realize that our thoughts and images come from our own personal storehouse of perceptions and experience, a collection of raw materials that is never quite the same for any two people.

For transmitting ideas or thoughts, a picture may indeed be worth a thousand words, but sometimes the best we can do is to paint a picture with words. We see the image clearly in our heads, but we forget that our words may not adequately convey the picture. Even a word as seemingly specific as "red" conveys a somewhat different image to each of us. The more specifics we use, the clearer the word painting becomes. Contrast the pictures painted by the phrases at the left (taken from the beginning of the section entitled "The Habit of Generality," page 27) with the more specific phrases to the right:

"I'm feeling a bit under the weather."	"My lower back is acting up again."
"You know, Joe's report seemed pretty good."	"Joe's report really gave all the pros and cons for each alternative."
"My line of work is sales."	"I sell pickles to the big supermarkets."
"We've just got to improve our communications with each other."	"You seem to nod your head as if you understand, and then you go off and do something different from what we agreed on."
"I just don't seem to have enough time."	"I must get thirty phone calls a day."

But often the specifics we need may not come readily to the tip of the tongue. We may have forgotten the specifics we originally used to build our idea. Or perhaps we never had all the specifics to begin with; we just picked up something from someone else that made sense to us without going back to the specifics. Even if we *know* all the specifics, it can take considerable effort to put them into words.

So getting specifics as well as giving them requires effort. The techniques that follow are described primarily from the point of view of getting the other person to be specific. Using the same approaches on yourself, however, can also help you be more specific.

> *We think in generalities, we live in detail.*
>
> —ALFRED NORTH WHITEHEAD

SPECIFIC TECHNIQUES

One of the best ways to push for specifics is so obvious as to be frequently overlooked: Simply ask straightforwardly for more specifics—with a phrase like one of these:

"Could you be more specific about . . . ?"

"Give me the details."

"Are you thinking of something in particular?"

With these phrases, as with most of the other techniques to follow, the more specifically you ask for specifics, the more specifics you'll get. For instance, suppose the other person is talking about a new kind of smoke detector he just had installed that is really terrific. Instead of just asking generally for more specifics, you can ask for details about the reliability of the detector, what makes it different from the others, how much it cost, and so on.

E.G.ing the Other Person On

Examples are nothing more than specific instances or samples that illustrate some broader, more general statement. So asking for examples is an easy way to push the other person into specifics. There's no real trick to getting an example; just ask for one! If you get tired of using the word "example," you can substitute one of these phrases:

"For instance [pause]?"
"Such as [pause]?"
"Like what [pause]?"

> *Having children is an* example *of a hereditary trait; if your parents didn't have any children, the chances are you won't either.*

Quantification Helps a Lot

"So it helps a lot, eh. *How much?*"

"Well, there are many things you can put numbers on."

"Okay, I'll buy that, but *how many?*"

"Oh, I suppose it depends on your skill at finding the appropriate figures, but frequently it's not that hard."

"But *how often* is 'frequently'?"

"I'd say most of the time."

"And that would be roughly *what percent* of the time?"

And so on.

Well, you get the idea of this somewhat surreal conversation. You can see how quantitative questions push the other person into specifics (unless the other person is as obstinate a generalist as the first character in the above dialogue).

Certainly not everything in life can be adequately described by numbers. Still, more of the time than we need to, we talk much like the primitive tribesmen who could count to three and who lumped anything larger together in the phrase *a lot.* Numbers supply a lot of specific information. There are totals and subtotals, averages, ratios and percents, probabilities and odds. You can always ask "How much?" "How many?" "How large?" "How far?" "How long?" "How often?"—and keep on asking until you get some sort of quantitative answer.

If you want to get more specific, you can always count on quantification to help!

Six Servants to Specificity

> *I keep six honest serving men*
> *(They taught me all I knew);*
> *Their names are What and Why*
>   *and When*
> *And How and Where and Who.*
> —RUDYARD KIPLING

This little quatrain is an old standby of business texts, law courses, and journalism manuals. The six one-word interrogatories can help you find out a lot about any subject—a lot of specifics. These six types of questions also possess some more subtle properties that are worth knowing about.

DON'T PUT "WHY" ON FIRST

You may remember that old Abbott and Costello sketch about the baseball team with the oddly named players. "Who" plays first base, "What" plays second base, and "I Don't Know" is on third base. Costello keeps asking Abbott "Who's on first?" and Abbott keeps replying, "Yes, that's right."

All of this is by way of an offbeat introduction to the observation that we often put "Why?" on first, way ahead of "Who?" or "What?"—and we shouldn't. Lest you get as confused as Costello did in the sketch, let me explain why not "Why?"

- Someone tells you he is feeling down in the mouth. You immediately ask, "Why?"
- Someone presents a plan or a decision. You may tend to ask first off, "Why?"

Now, what type of answer does a "why?" typically call for? A "why" question typically pushes the other person into providing a logical, rational explanation. The reason for this is that the answer to a "why?" is some sort of a "because" statement. As the word itself implies, a "*because*" typically deals with "causes," and the world of cause and effect is the world of reason and logic. Cause-and-effect thinking can certainly be productive in certain situations. The hard sciences use it a lot, as does mathematics. But cause-and-effect thinking is often much less useful when it comes to dealing with human, animate situations instead of rockets or rocks. The way we feel about something or what we believe in often has no simple, logical explanation. Wendell Johnson put it this way in his book, *Your Most Enchanted Listener:*

> Most relationships do not work only one way, even though we say they do. Every effect is also a cause, every cause an effect . . . everything is related to everything else and the cause of anything is everything—though language forms say only one thing affects another.

Thus, the real "why" of a human situation (if there is any) often lies buried in a kind of infinite regress of events. For example, you feel a particular way because your boss did something, and your boss did that something because of what his wife said at breakfast, and she said that at breakfast because. . . . The real "why" may be somewhat fuzzy, incomplete, and full of inconsistencies. None of this has any place in a cogent, rational explanation of something. The other person is subconsciously aware of all this and therefore will try to answer your "why?" with some sort of logical, reasonable "because." As a result you may get a perfectly logical-sounding explanation that does not truly reflect what is going on in the other person's head. You get what might be called pseudospecifics.

Often, then, you are better off getting more specifics about *what* the other person is thinking before asking about *why* they are thinking it. You may want to get more data, information, or background before moving on to the interpretations or defense of a position typically produced by a "why?"

*Why questions produce only pat
answers, defensiveness,
rationalizations, excuses, and the
delusion that an event can be
explained by a single cause. The why
does not discriminate purpose, origin,
or background.*

—FRITZ PERLS

"Who?" or "which?" can be good alternatives to "why?" as a
starting question. For example, ask "Who are you talking about?"
or "Which ones do you mean?" By starting with these questions
you at least clarify something about the specific individuals or
objects involved in what the other person is saying.

Another good starting point for more details is the question
"what?" For instance, you can ask something like this:

"What happened?"

"What do you mean by . . . ?"

"What did you (or someone else) do?"

The strategy behind the "what?" approach is simply this: *Get to
the act instead of the adjective.* For instance, if someone tells you he
knows a mean man, all you get is the adjective "mean." But if you
can get that other person to tell you *what* the man does that is
mean, that the man likes to hold his cat's feet over the hot fire,
then you have gotten to an act—an act that is pretty *mean*ing full.

So all in all, maybe Abbott and Costello weren't that far off
base when they put "Who" on first and "What" on second!

"HOW?" CAN HELP YOU FIND OUT "WHAT?"

If the other person is talking to you about something he wants,
he is likely to state it in terms of some sort of goal or outcome.
For example:

- "You ought to take off some weight."
- "We have to get this report out by Friday."
- "I've got to keep my expenses down."

If you ask, "How do I [or you] do that?" you push the other

person into describing more about achieving the goal or objective. For example:

"What do you want?"

"A chicken in every pot." (The firm is in the chicken business, needless to say.)

"How do we do that?"

"By growing fifteen percent a year."

"How?"

"By expanding sales coverage to every major U.S. city."

"How?"

"Let's start by opening a midwestern sales office in six months."

"How?"

Etc. . . .

You can see how asking "how?" tends to produce specifics beyond what you get from asking an initial "what?" In other situations the "how" question may be phrased a bit differently. For example:

"How did you arrive at that?" (or "How do you know?")

"How did that happen?"

Again Fritz Perls puts it nicely in *The Gestalt Approach:* "The how inquires into the structure of an event, and once the structure is clear all the whys are automatically answered." (Note that these uses of "how" are different from asking "How come?" or "How could that be?" Those expressions are really alternative ways of asking "Why?" and will result in much the same response as already discussed for "why" questions. Also these uses of "how?" are not the same as using a "how?" in quantitative types of questions such as "How many?" or "How much?")

"WHERE?" AND "WHEN?" ARE EVEN MORE SPECIFIC

Everything in the real world takes place in space and time, and each event has its unique space or time or both. Your sneeze of yesterday is not the same as the one today. Thus it is that asking "where?" or "when?" produces specifics in addition to those you may have gotten from asking "who?" "what?" or "how?" That is why these two interrogatories are such favorites of detectives and prosecuting attorneys, who often need to pin things down very precisely, for example, *"Where* were you *when* you noticed your necklace was missing?" For the same reasons, a thorough set of business (or even family) plans includes where and when future activities or events are supposed to take place.

THE "HOW?" IS "WHO?"

As was noted previously, "who?" is sometimes a good question to start with. But "who?" can also be an important question to end up with as well—after you've asked "what?" "how?" "where?" and "when?" Plans for action can be very detailed. They can spell out each step of what is to be done, along with a timetable for each event. Often, however, such plans leave out the "who." And usually, unless the plans specify *who* is going to do each task, somehow the plans never materialize. In any conversation about action, it is all too easy for each person to assume that the "who" is not himself, but someone else. In fact the greatest problem with any "how" is often finding the "who." (A similar phenomenon occurs as well when the conversation turns critical or complaining, that is, the "who" with the grievous flaw is certainly not us.)

Wiler's Law (whoever he was)

Nothing is impossible for the man who doesn't have to do it himself!

Find Out What It's Not

If you want to specify what is covered in a specific portion of a picture, there are two basic approaches. First you can ask about the objects *within* the designated area. The other approach is to detail what is *outside* the area, that is, what is not included within it. Each approach will provide you with additional specifics. To take another example, suppose you are discussing a new type of medical insurance with your agent. After he describes the coverage (what is included), you'll find out a lot of additional details by asking one or more of these questions:

"What types of cost are *not covered?*"

"Are there any special illnesses that are *excluded?*"

"What kinds of *exceptions* are mentioned?"

In other words, no proposal or statement ever covers everything or resolves all your problems or meets all your expectations. Asking about the limitations, the exceptions, or the conditions usually uncovers new details or at least clarifies what you already know. One of movie producer Sam Goldwyn's favorite oddball phrases was, "Include me out!" Finding out what something isn't is precisely the way to learn what is included out. Finding out what something isn't helps you know better what it is.

The "So What?" Approach

Another way to elicit more specifics is to ask about the *relevance* of what is being said to the general topic of the discussion: What is the relationship of the idea to the problem at hand? What impact would a particular action have on the situation? You may often feel as if the way to ask this is with a "So what?" but that is likely to sound somewhat sarcastic or imply that you don't care about what is being said. Even asking, "How is that relevant?" may still come off as something of a put-down. You can get the same sort of detail, however, by using one of these questions instead:

"What is the *effect* of that on . . . ?"

"What kinds of *results* [or *outcome*] do you anticipate?"

"And then [pause]?"

The Techniques in Action

Here's a somewhat abbreviated conversation that illustrates most of the techniques discussed so far. Ordinarily you probably would not use as many of the techniques as Jack does in this particular example. Nonetheless, the sample conversation does let you see how each technique elicits a different kind of specific detail.

Sample Dialogue—To Illustrate Use of the Techniques for
Getting Down to Specifics

Comment

PETE: I understand you're
thinking of buying a second
car. You know you really
ought to go talk to the
Bendek Agency. They're
terrific.

JACK: What do you mean,
"terrific"?

starts with a "what"
question that gets to the
act instead of the
adjective

PETE: Well, I ended up with a lot
of extras thrown in that
didn't cost me anything.

JACK: Hmmm. Like what, for
example?

asks for an example

PETE: Oh, they didn't charge me
for the FM-AM radio, just
the regular cost of the
standard AM. And they
gave me a good deal on my
old car.

JACK: That sounds really good.
How much did you get for
that old clunker?

pushes for quantification

PETE: Let me see. I guess they knocked about seven hundred bucks off the new-car purchase price.

JACK: Tell me, Pete, how did all this come about?

asks "how?" in order to find out more about the "what"

PETE: See, this buddy of mine at work—you know Joe Roberts, don't you?—well, he has a couple of contacts over at Bendek and he set things up for me. Told 'em to take good care of me.

JACK: So who did you deal with there? Anyone in particular?

asks "who?" to find out about specific individuals

PETE: Yeah, Joe had me deal with Henry, who is sort of their senior salesman. A really nice guy.

JACK: What was the effect of that on your dealings?

asks about the relevance of the previous comment, that is, the "so what?" approach

PETE: Henry? Oh, he's been around and he knew the answers to most of my questions. And he didn't try any of those cutesy selling tactics on me.

JACK: I see. You know, I was just realizing you've had your car for a little while now. When exactly did you go through all this?

pins things down further by asking a "when?" question

PETE: Must have been about six months ago by now. It was a good time, too, because business was slow for them, and they were anxious to move some cars.

JACK: Sounds like I should at least talk to them. Now, do I contact them direct, or do you want to talk to Joe or . . . ?

asks "who?" again, this time to get details on how to proceed, i. e., the "how" is "who"

PETE: Tell you what. Let me talk to Joe and have him find out what's what over there now, and then I'll get back to you.

JACK: Great, great. But, you know, there was one thing I was wondering. Was there anything you didn't like about the way Bendek dealt with you?

asks what it (Bendek) is not, now that he knows something about what it is

PETE: Not really. Of course they
did the usual bit of trying
to trade me up to a more
expensive model, but I
wasn't having any of that.
And they didn't have the
car ready for me when they
said they would. But
nothing major.

JACK: Hey, Pete, I appreciate your
going through all this with
me. I'll talk to you in a
couple of days on this after
you've seen Joe. Take it
easy.

The Second Effort (and More)

One of the atypical things about the preceding sample conversation is that Pete did come up with some real specifics in answer to each of Jack's questions. Usually the first response to a probing question is far too general, no matter whether it's an organization problem-solving session, a seminar discussion, or a household debate. For example:

"When are you going to take care of that leaky faucet, dear?"
"I've got it on my list, don't worry."

"Could you tell me specifically what kinds of work you handle?"
"Well, it's hard to generalize. You know, I take care of a wide variety of situations."

"How do you think we can improve this productivity problem?"
"Well, one thing we need is to get the men more motivated."

You may be tempted to think that it is the wording of your probes that causes the lack of specificity in the initial response.

But as the examples illustrate, no matter which approach you use first and no matter how cooperative the other person wishes to be, you'll probably have to probe several times before you get the level of specificity you want. The reasons for this phenomenon probably go back to the habit of generality or the lack of understanding or to fear on the part of the other person about what you are really getting at. So be prepared to make the second effort (and sometimes more).

The only thing you have to watch out for is that in your zeal to get down to specifics you do not make the other person feel she is undergoing a third degree. *Presenting your reasons for wanting to know more* is one good way of taking the curse off your pushing for specifics. And, incidentally, "curiosity" is usually not a very good reason to present. When you say, "I'm just curious," the phrase tends to be interpreted as meaning you have a damn-good reason but you're just not willing to say what it is. Naturally, such an interpretation can inhibit your getting the specifics you want.

The point is still that no matter which of the techniques in this chapter you use, you must be prepared to probe in a specific direction at least several times before arriving at the most useful level of specificity. Which brings us to one last important issue.

HOW SPECIFIC DO YOU NEED TO GET?

The bad news is that "levels of specificity" is a tricky subject to discuss. A "level" is hard to specify, and the most effective level of specificity varies with each conversation. You can get too specific and hung up in the details as well as getting too general.

The good news is that it is relatively easy to know when you are at the right level of specificity because things suddenly become clear, that is, you understand or you know how to do what is needed.

In order for you to get a clearer idea of what "levels of specificity" means, try the series of experiments in the following exercise.

What Level of Specificity Feels Right to You?

Read down each series of statements below and put a check mark beside the statement that causes you to have a reaction similar to the one quoted to the right of each series.

1. A description
☐ A. "Imagine my dog;
☐ B. he's a Saint Bernard;
☐ C. that is, a baby Saint Bernard;
☐ D. but he's mostly brown;
☐ E. with a white collar and a white spot on his nose."

"Yeah, now I can visualize that pretty well."

2. A problem
☐ A. "Avoid overspending;
☐ B. especially on office costs;
☐ C. I mean our phone bill is out of sight;
☐ D. and our operator can't refuse to place calls."

"I get the picture and I've got a couple of ideas about what we might try."

3. An evaluation
☐ A. "He's just insubordinate;
☐ B. that is, he avoids responsibility;
☐ C. like his attendance record;
☐ D. you know, he stops work about an hour early every day;
☐ E. and I'm told he walks home when the weather is nice;
☐ F. and sometimes he stops in the park."

"Oh, I see what you mean, although I'm not sure it's all necessarily bad."

4. An action
- [ ] A. "Pay more attention to
  her;
- [ ] B. that is, spend more time   "Sure, I can see how to
  with her;   do that!"
- [ ] C. for example, have her over
  to your house;
- [ ] D. maybe for dinner;
- [ ] E. and you could have a nice
  seafood meal;
- [ ] F. and talk about classical
  music."

Many people checked these boxes:
   1-E   3-D
   2-C   4-D

Whether or not you checked those same boxes is not really relevant. The point is that most people who went through these little experiments did feel a clear little "ping" when they reached a certain statement in each series; and their reading of the further statements usually confirmed the original ping (even though not everyone felt the ping at the same place in a particular series of statements).

For instance, in series #4 few people felt the need to be told what to have for dinner when inviting over the woman; they felt that the idea of dinner was sufficiently specific. On the other hand, a few people did find it helpful to have some information about the woman's preferences. Naturally the "right" level of specificity varies a good deal with what you already know and also with what action or reaction is needed in the particular discussion. If someone asks you to tie a knot and then specifies a square knot, that may be sufficient; but if you missed Basic Knots 101 in the Boy Scouts or Campfire Girls, then you may need a lot more specifics. But how much detail you need about the knot to tie also depends on whether you are just tying together two pieces of clothesline or tying a sailboat up to a dock.

In any case, when you seem to be stymied in a discussion, try changing the level of specificity. *Consciously move one level up* (more general) and see how it feels; *or move one level down* (less general) and see if that unlocks the conversation. You'll be surprised by how quickly you know whether you're moving in the right direction. Whether you are describing, problem finding, analyzing, criticizing, helping, or instructing, the right level of specificity can do wonders for improving the productivity of the discussion.

> *Sometimes we can't see the forest for the trees. But just as often we can't see the trees for the forest.*

3 Committing Tolerable Criticism

'Tis better to give than to receive.

Most people would rather defend to the death your right to say it than listen to it.

—ROBERT BRAULT

There's a story, well known in musical circles, about the great English conductor Sir Thomas Beecham. The late Sir Thomas was attending a performance of Verdi's opera *Aïda*, in which there is a marvelous triumphal procession where a great variety of elephants, horses, and other animals troup onto the stage.

It seems this particular performance of *Aïda* was rather uninspired, and to top it all off, right at the climax of the triumphal procession one of the horses received an urgent call from mother nature. Right in the middle of the stage the horse dumped his load.

After the performance a newpaper reporter asked Sir Thomas what he thought of the incident with the horse. Sir Thomas replied, "Well, he's not much of an actor, but, egad, what a critic!"

THE CRITICAL PROBLEM

"Gee, mom, I really feel great. You should have heard the criticism I got today in school."

"I sure feel brilliant now that you've told me what's wrong with my idea."

"I can tell you love me—by the way you disagree so violently with my opinions."

Do these phrases sound a bit unfamiliar? Sure they do! We aren't very likely to hear them—unless we've got some very sarcastic acquaintances.

In this chapter, "criticism" means "disagreement or disapproval, negative judgments, fault finding." Now, which of the following reactions would another person be likely to feel as a result of being criticized?

- ☐ A. rejected or unloved
- ☐ B. dumb or stupid
- ☐ C. worthless or inadequate
- ☐ D. powerless or helpless
- ☐ E. more confused than before

How about all of the above!

Most of us view our ideas and opinions (and even our information) as parts of our selves, as extensions of our very personal identity. So, often criticism makes the person receiving it feel that his individual worth is being impugned, and that person is likely to feel angry or unhappy or both.

Love me, love my dogma.

Criticism also creates other problems or obstacles for the person receiving it. If the criticism shows the other person that his information or opinion is wrong, then he must somehow reorganize his thinking, and that can mean changing around a lot of things in his head. If his idea has some fatal flaw, he must expend time and energy to come up with a new idea or to find a way around the flaw.

We often feel that *giving* criticism *brings* something to the other person—a gift we bestow. In reality, we are usually taking something away: either a part of his personal worth or a part of some desired goal or a part of the plan to reach that goal. We are erecting barriers that block his path.

> *Nobody likes the bringer of bad news.*
> —SOPHOCLES

Does all this mean there is no place for criticism? Why bother criticizing anybody in the first place? The critical problem arises precisely because criticism can have great value. Criticism is a way to help people we care for or feel responsible for, a way to help them solve or avoid problems. Criticism helps people learn from their mistakes and their experience; it is a way to improve their performance. Criticism is an important part of testing out ideas and perfecting them. Criticism is a way for us to exert our influence, to shape and mold the world around us toward what we believe is better or more appropriate.

And does the other person really want us to accept everything he says, not just as a matter of form but honestly to agree with him and act on what he says? Wouldn't the other person find life quite dull if he never expected (and never received) any criticism?

Well, of course, the other person (the one receiving the criticism) is often us, and most of us would agree that in theory being criticized can be useful and meaningful. But in actuality what most of us want is only the *possibility* of being criticized. We don't want a guaranteed win. We would like to feel that others had the option of criticizing us, but would choose not to exercise it. (It's a bit like the old theory of morality: Without the possibility of evil, how can man make the moral choice between good and evil?)

All right, so the world is probably a better (or at least a more interesting) place with criticism than without it. Even if we are on the receiving end of the criticism, we have to admit that it brings substantial payoffs. But that doesn't mean we like it or look forward to it:

> Even if we really want it,
> we pray we won't get it.

> When we get it,
> even if we agree with it,
> we wish it weren't so.

In a nutshell, here's what all this means for us in the role of criticism givers. We are not going to stop giving criticism. It's just too valuable and important. But we must not expect the criticism we give to be enthusiastically embraced. The best we can hope for is that our criticism will be accepted as tolerable. And making our criticism more tolerable is what the rest of this chapter is about.

> *A diplomat is a person who can tell
> you to go to hell in such a way that
> you actually look forward to the trip.*
> —CASKIE STINNETT

TECHNIQUES TO MAKE YOUR CRITICISM MORE TOLERABLE

Understand First, Criticize Later

Chapter 1 described the most common responses for filling in the blank in this statement:

> When I discuss an issue with someone else, I wish that he or she would _____.

You will recall that many of the answers indicated a desire for the other person to really listen or understand. Each of the people who responded to this question was then immediately asked to complete the following phrase:

> When I disagree with what someone is saying, the first thing I do is _____.

Here are some of the typical responses for this statement:

- "Tell 'em I disagree, but nicely."
- "Suggest that they analyze what they are saying."
- "Frown!"
- "Consider the viewpoint, and if it is sound in my judgment, then use the idea."
- "Wait for the opportunity to present my point of view."
- "Say, 'You may have a point; however, have you thought about this solution?' "
- "Collect my thoughts and prepare a rebuttal."

What suddenly happened to the importance of listening and understanding, which not a minute before had been emphasized by so many of these same people? Perhaps this inconsistency just illustrates the big difference between wanting to be understood and being willing to understand someone else. In any case, it is all too easy to forget the importance of understanding the other person's point of view. And you risk double or triple jeopardy if you ignore this most important thing when you are criticizing: *Prove you understand before you criticize.*

The scene is a meeting of the Customer Relations Group of the Wixstel Company. The background is that Wixstel customers have been making an increasing number of complaints about the products. As part of an overall company program to deal with this complaint situation, the executive vice-president has asked the Customer Relations Group to think about what actions the group itself could take. After some initial discussion of the complaint problem, Cary volunteers an idea.

CARY: So anyway, what I think we ought to do is get out a monthly bulletin to the sales and service managers. And what we'd do is report on the various types of complaints we've been hearing about from all the different places. This way the managers would become aware of the complaints and how frequent they are, and they could take appropriate action in their own areas.

JANE: Well, I don't know. You remember how we used to write up different customer problems in the company newsletter, and that didn't seem to help very much and it took a lot of time.

In this example Jane responds as if she knows what Cary is talking about—always a dangerous procedure. As it turns out, Cary and Jane are really talking about two different things. Later on in the discussion Cary makes clear that what she is thinking about is a kind of statistical report; whereas Jane seems to be thinking more of a collection of anecdotes. Cary and Jane could end up arguing for quite a while to little purpose because each of them would be talking about different ideas.

So check out your understanding first before you jump in with your criticism. Your only risk in clarifying what the other person is saying is that by the time you fully understand her position, your original criticism may no longer seem valid. (For more on clarifying and proving your understanding, refer back to pages 14–20.) Your most skilled and tactful criticism will be tolerable only if the other person first believes she has been understood!

Don't Be Objective*

SAM: I gather, Cary, what you're really talking about is almost like a statistical report that would list the major types of complaints and how many of each we're getting. Right?

CARY: Exactly, and I think our people could really do a lot on the basis of that kind of information.

SAM: Yeah, but these things always sound great and then somehow they never accomplish very much. It's just another report, and nobody's going to pay much attention to it.

We all tend to feel more secure about criticizing if we have "right" or "truth" on our side.

So we often try to bolster our criticism by stating it as if it were "factual," as if it were an objective statement with which nobody in his right mind could disagree. This is precisely what Sam is doing here in his second statement, albeit subtly. (But give Sam credit for checking out his understanding first, before launching into his criticism.)

The problem is that "facts" and "the truth" and "what is right" tend to be very personal and subjective. The facts of yesterday may be false today. What is true for you may not be so for me. What is right in one situation may not be so in another.

The truth of the matter (if indeed there be any truth at all) is that any criticism is always just an opinion.

There are two sides to every
argument, until you take one.
                    —LAURENCE J. PETER

*Pun fully intended.

It is very hard for another person to accept that what he has said is wrong, false, or untrue and that other person will usually fight like crazy to escape such an implication. But you may create even worse trouble if you should succeed in convincing the other person that he has said something wrong, false, or untrue. Your success is likely to cause the other person to feel "bad" or "one down" or "inferior" or "not okay." And that other person won't like feeling this way. His natural reaction will probably be to try to get back at you somehow, if not right now, then later on in the discussion; or else he may just withdraw his energy completely from the discussion.

So try to think of the other person's words or actions by themselves as neutral, that is, neither good nor bad, neither true nor untrue. It is *you* who supplies the judgment or evaluation. Try stating your criticism as a personal view, as *your* reaction or feeling, not as "right" or the "truth." Start off with something like this:

"In my opinion . . ."
"The way I see it is . . ."
"I feel that . . ."

What this technique does is to give the other person an escape hatch, a way out. If what you express is *just* your opinion, then certainly the other person is entitled to have his opinion. Another kind of escape hatch is to couch your criticism in such conditional terms as these:

"Sometimes . . ."
"Maybe . . ."
"Possibly . . ."

In any case, try not to set up your conversation as a battle between right and wrong, between truth and falsehood, between fact and fiction. What you say (as well as what the other person says) isn't any of these things—it's just a personal opinion, even if you believe in it very strongly. (For more on personalizing, see chapter 7.)

Okay, it's just my opinion. . . . But
I think you're dead wrong!

> *Generally the theories we believe we call facts, and the facts we disbelieve we call theories.*
>
> ——FELIX COHEN

Don't Get Personal

CARY: I don't say that the bulletin will be the magic cure. We'd probably have to spend some time talking with some of the sales and service managers to make sure they understand the report and know how to use it. But I think we can do it.

JANE: Oh, come on, Cary, you're always so overly optimistic about the effectiveness of this kind of thing.

No matter how carefully it is worded, any *criticism is always an attack.*

Jane's comment makes a statement about Cary as a person, not just about her idea. That is, Cary *is* "overly optimistic." It's bad enough to attack the other person's dogma, but a direct assault on the other person's self is usually quite intolerable. So criticize what the other person *says* or *does,* not what the other person is. To make your criticism more tolerable, *criticize the opinion, idea, or action, not the person.*

Less-Tolerable Examples	*More-Tolerable Examples*
"From my point of view, you don't think things through very carefully."	"I see some serious inconsistencies in your position."

"I feel you're being too conservative."

"I don't think that suggestion will change things as much as I would like."

"I think you're plain lazy, that's what I think."

"I'm really mad you didn't do those errands I asked you to do."

(Note that both sets of examples are stated as personal opinions. But there is still a difference between the left-hand set, which criticizes the person, and the right-hand set, which criticizes the idea, opinion, or action.)

Criticize Process as well as (or instead of) Content

When anyone says or does something, there are two different elements to which you can react. First, there is the *way* in which the thing was said or done, that is, the process or procedures followed. Second, there is the content of what was said or done. Usually when you are upset about what somebody has said or done, *process is what really bothers you,* but *content is what gets talked about.* Here are a few examples that clarify the distinction between process and content:

1. An employee turns in a report late to his boss.

   The boss chews out the employee because the boss says he needed the report for a meeting at the end of the week, and now he has very little time to study it. — Content

   What is really steaming the boss, however, is that the subordinate gave him no warning that the report might be late, and then the fellow just left the report on his desk with no apology or other comment. — Process

2. As they are getting dressed for dinner, a husband suddenly informs his wife that they are meeting some friends at an Italian restaurant instead of going out alone to the local delicatessen as they had planned.

The wife complains about having to dress differently and grumbles about the choice of restaurant and "having to make conversation with the friends."

Content

What is really upsetting the wife is that her husband waited until they were dressing to announce the change in plans. He ought to have at least seen fit to discuss the change with her and give her a chance to voice her own opinion, even though, as it happens, the Italian restaurant is one of her favorites and the friends are people she really likes to see.

Process

3. At the meeting of the Wixstel Customer Relations Group, Cary is pushing for her complaint bulletin idea. At one point she says, "And I'm sure Jennifer would have some time to help pull together the figures, wouldn't you, Jenny?" Jenny replies in a fairly noncommittal way.

After the meeting Jennifer pulls Cary aside, and with considerable annoyance in her voice says, "Look, I think the bulletin is a good idea, but you knew I was in the middle of having my house redecorated, and I've just started putting together this training program for our salesmen. I mean, how could I possibly have any extra time?"   Content

What Jenny is really boiling about is the way in which Cary volunteered Jenny's services without leaving Jenny a graceful way out.   Process

In each of these cases what is being criticized is mostly the content of what happened. Since the content was only a part of the issue (and in the case of the husband and wife perhaps not even an issue at all), criticizing just the content leaves both parties rather unsettled. The person criticized doesn't really understand what was wrong, and the person doing the criticizing doesn't really deal with what is upsetting him the most. The result often can be an acrimonious discussion, with accusations flying back and forth. Even worse, the same situation may easily recur, because the real source of upset has not been identified or discussed.

In other words in the three examples above, there is no reason why the boss or the wife or Jennifer couldn't have said something about the material identified in the margin as "process," instead of just talking about the material identified in the margin as "content." And there is a nice bonus you get from focusing your criticism on the process part of what the other person has said or done: Most people will usually find your criticism more tolerable if it emphasizes process rather than content.

Be Specific

Any criticism is always an attack.

> Sam: Yeah, but these things always sound great, and
> then somehow they never accomplish very much.
>
> Jane: Oh, come on, Cary, you're always so overly opti-
> mistic.

General criticism is in some ways like a general bombing raid
that wipes out a whole city, which must then be rebuilt from
scratch. It tends to wipe out totally the other person's idea. What
is valuable gets destroyed right along with what is less valuable.
Yet almost everything someone says has *some* value, at least to the
person saying it. So, general criticism is particularly intolerable.

Specific criticism is more like precision, pinpoint bombing. You
destroy one or two strategic targets, which may still cause a lot
of anguish, but the rest of the city can survive and continue to
function.

The point of these analogies is not to suggest that you should
view a conversation in this context as a hostile adversary situation. It is used rather to capture the sense of attack typically felt
by the recipient of criticism.

Cary will have a tough time defending herself against the general criticisms leveled at her in the Customer Relations Group
meeting—"These things . . . never accomplish very much" and
"you're always so overly optimistic." Such criticisms often cause
the discussion to degenerate into the typical "'tis-'tisn't" or "yes,
you will–no, I won't" argument.

Suppose Sam or Jane were to focus their criticism by adding
one or more of these specifics:

1. The sales and service managers won't know how to interpret
   all that statistical data.
2. It would take us four to five man-days a month to put the report together and talk personally with the managers about it.

3. The service managers already know about most of the complaints, and the sales managers can't do much about the problems anyway.

These specifics don't say that the *whole* bulletin idea is ridiculous. Furthermore, Cary can defend herself against such a specific if she is so inclined. For example, in response to the first specific, Cary could suggest ways of designing the bulletin to help the managers interpret the data. Or in response to the second specific she could indicate why she feels the report would not take that much time to handle. Even if Cary does not or cannot provide an answer to these specific criticisms, perhaps someone else at the meeting will do so.

> *A vague idea may avoid irritating others, but not a vague criticism.*

ONE THING AT A TIME

Destroying just one small area with pinpoint bombing gives a city the chance to rebuild that area or else to shift around its pattern of activity to compensate for the lost area. But if a number of individually bombed areas are all decimated at once, the results again begin to resemble those of a general raid.

Thus, one important part of being specific is to *criticize one thing at a time.* By doing this you give the other person a better chance to cope: to argue against your criticism; to develop alternatives for dealing with the problem you raise; to think through the new ideas triggered by your criticism; to readjust the rest of his thinking to compensate for the damage done. A number of business firms have formally incorporated something of this philosophy into their employee appraisal procedures. These firms limit the number of negative items to be covered during any one appraisal session to no more than two or three. The managers in these firms have found that an employee simply cannot emotionally accept more than a couple of faults or problems at a time; and also it is apparently difficult for an employee to work subsequently on improving more than a couple of deficiencies.

Even in a conversation that is less critically oriented, psychologist Jesse Nirenberg recommends not speaking for more than twenty seconds if you really want the listener to absorb what you are saying. Obviously, critical comments are especially difficult for the other person to absorb.

Okay, but what do you do with all the other faults or problems you see in what the other person has said or done? The simple answer is just to pick out the one or two items you feel are most crucial and let the rest go for the moment. Perhaps you can bring them up later in the discussion or in some later discussion. (Although you should beware of dragging out one criticism after another, that is, just when the other person has responded to one criticism, you introduce another and so on.) Most of the time you will find that once you focus in on the most important specific criticism, your other concerns may disappear or change significantly. In other words, once you talk through a specific concern, clarify it, understand more about why the other person said or did what he did—perhaps work on ways to alleviate your concern— then you will find that the nature of the situation has often changed enough to minimize or invalidate your other points of criticism.

In any case, if you criticize too many things all at once, you are very likely to overpower or totally discourage the other person. Even if each of your critical comments is highly specific, the odds are that an all-at-once approach will not prove very tolerable. Of course, if your intent is completely to incapacitate or paralyze the other person . . .

NEVER SAY "NEVER" OR "ALWAYS"

In one sense the words "never" and "always" can be considered very precise, but at the same time they are not very specific; they refer to past, present, and future without distinction. And these words are rarely accurate, since they do not allow for any exceptions, and there are usually exceptions to almost everything. For instance, Cary is probably not always as overly optimistic as Jane claims (that is, assuming she is even being overly optimistic at the moment).

There are a number of other similar words it pays to avoid, such as "everything," "totally," "constantly," "every time." All these words subtly push the discussion from a specific issue into the question of whether or not a larger generalization is valid. For example, Sam's statement that "these things . . . never accomplish very much" is likely to lead Cary into arguing the truth of that general assertion: Cary will try to prove that sometimes these things *do* work out well.

All-encompassing words, such as "never" and "always," tend to batten down all the escape hatches pretty tightly, and that can make the other person pretty angry or at least highly intolerant of your criticism. A better approach can be to qualify your critical observations in one of these ways:

"When you said (or did) . . . I felt . . ."

"Right now I feel you are . . ."

"In this specific instance it seems to me . . ."

> *"What, never?"*
> *"No, never!"*
> *"What, never?"*
> *"Well, hardly ever."*
> ——W. S. GILBERT

CRITICISM TO SOME EFFECT

So the sales managers won't know how to interpret the statistical data in the complaint report, or so it will take four to five man-days a month to handle the report—so what? What is the point? What that is undesirable will happen as a result?

By including the answers to this kind of question in your criticism, you clarify considerably what you are really concerned about. The other person is not left guessing at what you are trying to get at. By saying something about the undesirable consequences or effects that follow from your critical observation, you are, essentially, making your criticism much more specific.

Just think of finishing your critical observation with one of these phrases:

"Therefore . . ."

"So . . ."

"As a result . . ."

Here are some examples of negative effects that might have been mentioned in connection with the specific criticisms suggested back on page 58 about the complaint bulletin idea:

Specific Criticisms	*Negative Effects or Impact*
1. The sales and service managers won't know how to interpret all that statistical data."	"Therefore, the managers won't bother to read the report." or "So, the managers won't know what actions to take."
2. It would take us four to five man-days a month to put the report together and talk personally with the managers about it."	"Therefore, we would have to drop some of the projects we are working on now." or "As a result, we would end up spending some money for overtime work, and we aren't budgeted for that."
3. "The service managers already know about most of the complaints, and the sales managers can't do very much about the problems anyway."	"So even if the report is read, it won't improve the complaint situation very much."

When you describe the undesirable consequences, you help the other person better understand your thinking, and you may even convince her that your criticism is not entirely capricious. Stating the effect or impact also *promotes viewing the dis-*

cussion in problem-solving terms. For instance, by stating that "managers won't bother to read the report," the subsequent discussion can address itself to figuring out ways to make the report more readable. And notice that dealing with this issue is somewhat different from dealing with the issue of managers not knowing what actions to take (even if they do read the report). Yet both these negative effects could flow from the same specific criticism about sales and service managers not knowing how to interpret statistical data.

Of course, you have a right to be unsure of why you don't like something. You are entitled to make capricious criticisms, or you may choose to hide your real concerns. You may even choose to criticize out of anger or in retaliation to the other person's previous criticism of you. In such cases, you will probably find it hard to be specific and explain the effects or impact of your critical observations. On the other hand, you can hardly then expect the other person to be very tolerant of your criticism.

Criticism is a call to action.

Where's the Action?
Any criticism is a way of asking for change. Indirectly (or directly) you are asking the other person to

- drop his idea
- modify his opinion
- behave differently

But change implies action—by you or the other person or both of you. And the other person typically senses that the implication of action lies behind any criticism.

At the very least, the other person will be concerned with what action you may be planning to take. Are you going to fire (or divorce) him, punish him, stop discussing anything with him, just reject his idea, help him deal with your criticism, or what? So don't wait too long to get into the action implications of your criticism, otherwise the other person may get so concerned about what *you* are planning to do that he won't hear the rest of what you are saying.

Now, to make your criticism as tolerable as possible, the action you will probably want to take is to help the other person deal with your criticism. A good approach for doing this is to *put your criticism into a problem-solving framework*. By doing this you imply your interest in discussing action alternatives rather than dwelling on the finality of your critical opinion. Try ending your criticism with this phrase: "So from my point of view, *the problem is how to* . . ."* You could, of course, go further and *suggest some specific alternatives for action.*

For instance, in the Wixstel Company situation, suppose that Sam had made the specific criticism about the managers not knowing how to interpret all the statistical data in the complaint bulletin being proposed by Cary. And suppose Sam had gone on to point out that therefore the managers wouldn't bother to read the report. Sam could then have finished by saying, "So from my point of view the problem is how to put together a report that the managers will want to read and will be able to understand easily." Or Sam could have gone on to propose a few possibilities for action, such as putting the report on audiotape so that the managers could listen to it at their leisure, or including some written analysis of the figures right in the report so that the key points would be easy to spot. (Notice that in these examples of possible action alternatives the *benefit* of the action is also stated. Generally, it is a good idea to do this. State the way your action idea would help solve the problem posed by your criticism.)

Taking an action orientation in your criticism is particularly important, because your criticism is not only an opinion but also a *judgment*. In a courtroom trial, the only action a defendant can take against the court's judgment is to appeal the verdict. And that is exactly what the victim of your criticism is likely to do.

*As far as I know, this italicized phrase was developed by Synectics, Inc., a firm that works in the area of creative problem solving (located in Cambridge, Mass.).

He will literally appeal your "sentence"; he will argue against the verdict or perhaps consider taking the case to a higher authority. What else can he do—*unless you open up the discussion to other possibilities for action?* Notice that by suggesting alternatives you lessen the emphasis on the judgmental character of your criticism and focus more on the action implications of what you are saying. Besides, remember that a criticism, even if stated as a problem, still takes something away from the other person. It seems only fair that you try to give him something in return.

Of course, if you state a problem on which very little action is possible, your criticism won't be very tolerable. For example, a basketball coach is criticizing one of his players for not getting enough rebounds and says, "So from my point of view the problem is how to make you six inches taller. Any ideas?"

It is precisely for this same reason that criticizing past performance is always tricky: There is little action anyone can take to alter the past. This doesn't mean that you can't discuss how to make the future different from the past, how to deal with the present results of something that occurred in the past. But the only opportunity for action lies always in the present or future.

> *Think like a man of action, act like a man of thought.*
>
> —HENRI BERGSON

> *Don't throw the baby out with the bathwater.*
>
> —ANONYMOUS

IT CAN'T BE ALL BAD

The previous section described a number of techniques for expressing what you don't like about the other person's ideas or actions, and certainly most ideas and actions have some serious defects. There are few perfect answers.

But consider the other side of the coin. Most people don't go about muttering thoughts or taking actions they believe to be utterly inane. If you don't find anything worthwhile in what the other person says or does, you are in essence making him out to be something of an idiot—which is hardly the way to make your criticism tolerable, no matter what you say. At best, the other person will feel that you didn't listen carefully enough to understand fully what he said.

Since the other person is quite likely to feel there *is* something valuable in what he is saying, then *you* become the dullard for not being able to find it. In short, if you don't find something of merit in the other person's ideas or actions, then *one of you is an idiot.* And much of your subsequent discussion will be devoted to establishing exactly which one of you it is.

Besides, when you throw away *all* of an idea (your own or that of someone else), you end up continually restarting from ground zero. And continually building from scratch is laborious. You risk not building anything at all. By seeking out the useful parts of what the other person says, you provide both of you with the chance to build on something. And then you can both work on the inevitable defects; work on them as problems to be solved, with neither one of you cast in the role of village idiot.

> *Okay, for the sake of argument, let's assume you know what you're talking about.*
>
> —BILL HOEST

What all this means is that it is a good idea to *include some credits along with your criticism,* no matter how you word the criticism. In reacting to another person's ideas or actions, you need to cover your likes as well as your dislikes, your agreements as well as your disagreements, the pluses as well as the minuses, the pros as well as the cons. If you don't comment on both sides of the coin, then your chances of committing tolerable criticism are very low.

> ### It Really Happened
>
> During a meeting, Harry says to Joe, "That idea of yours really stinks."
>
> The leader reminds Harry about the importance of saying what you like as well as what you don't like about an idea.
>
> Harry replies, "That's what I like! Now let me tell you my criticism."

Use "And" Instead of "But" Phrases

If you are going to mix in credits with your criticism, watch out for the subtle, powerful difference between doing so with "but" phrases instead of "and" phrases. If you are not careful, a "but" phrase becomes an all-purpose eraser. Fritz Perls, in his book *The Gestalt Approach,* uses this example to make the point:

Mother says, "He's ugly, *but* he's very rich."

Daughter says, "He's very rich, *but* he's ugly."

The mother is really saying it is not all that important that he is ugly; what is really significant is that he is rich. The daughter, of course, is saying just the opposite. The point is that the "but" tends to signal a lack of significance in what comes before the "but." Here are a few more typical examples of using a "but" phrase to mix credits with criticism:

"Joe's a nice guy and all that, but he always irritates the people he works with."

"That's a great idea, but I just don't think it would work out in practice."

Do you see how the "but" phrase signals that the first stuff was just fluff or filler, a token attempt to say something nice before really laying on the hard-nosed criticism? You recognize the "but" signal, and so will the other person.

> *Diplomacy is the art of saying, "Nice doggie!" till you can find a rock.*
> —WYNN CATLIN

Now, you may feel that these examples are biased, that not all "but" phrases erase what comes before as thoroughly as these. And that's probably true, because the examples were chosen to highlight the character of "but" phrases. Even in less extreme examples, however, you can still notice the same effect of the "but" phrase:

> "You know, I think your report has gathered and organized a lot of good data, but I don't agree with the conclusions you reached."

> "I appreciate your having picked up all the stuff off the floor in your room, but your drawers are still in a mess."

Do you see how these examples still tend to downplay the credit that comes before the "but"?

Here are some of the same credits and criticisms expressed using some sort of "and" phrase:

> "What I like about your report is the data you've gathered and organized, and what I have a problem with is the conclusions you've reached."

> "I'm pleased that you picked up all the stuff off the floor in your room, and I'm not so pleased that your drawers are still in a mess."

Notice how the mixture of credits and criticism somehow come across as much more evenhanded. You may notice that the wording in this second set of examples has been altered somewhat beyond just substituting "and" for "but." That is correct, and it is precisely the point. Thinking about using an "and" phrase forces you to deal much more explicitly with the existence of both sides, pro and con, useful and not so useful. You automatically find yourself reworking what you say to utilize such phrasings as these:

"On the one hand . . . and on the other hand . . ."

"What I agree with is . . . and what I disagree with is . . ."

"What I like is . . . and what I don't like is . . ."

Thinking in terms of "and" by no means guarantees equal weighting to credits and criticism, nor should that be necessarily what you are striving for. By thinking "and" instead of "but," however, what you say is much more likely to convey that *both your credits and your criticism are relevant and important.* Basically nothing is all good or all bad; everything is good *and* bad. The bad may outweigh the good (or vice versa), but the one doesn't cancel out the other; they both continue to exist!

Just start by listening to the use of the word "but" as it pops up in the conversation of others, and see the way it affects the conversation. Soon you will begin noticing your own use of "but" phrases. Simply by keeping the distinction between "but" and "and" in your mind, you will probably find yourself expressing your mix of credits and criticism a little bit differently—and a lot more tolerably.

> *Anyone who agrees with you in principle is probably preparing to tell you how wrong you are.*
> —FRANKLIN P. JONES

> *To speak ill of others is a dishonest way of praising ourselves.*
> —WILL DURANT

SUMMARY—THE CRITICAL PATH

The summary chart at the end of this chapter puts all the techniques for committing tolerable criticism in one place for easy reference. At this point, however, you may be say yourself, "Good heavens, how can I ever remember all that? Do I really have to use all of those techniques every time I criticize somebody?" The answer is you probably won't remember all of the techniques, nor will you use all of them all the time.

The nice part of committing tolerable criticism is that it is not an all-or-nothing matter. Using just one of the techniques will make your criticism *more* tolerable than it otherwise might have been. The more techniques you use, the more tolerable your criticism will be, but you don't have to use all of them before there will be a noticeable difference.

So pick one or two of the techniques that seem most congenial to you, and try them out. You'll find that many of the techniques are related, that is, using one or two of them naturally leads to using some of the others, without much conscious effort on your part. The fact is that all the techniques relate to the same particular state of mind, a state of mind best illuminated by this anecdote from a book called *The Only Dance There Is* by Baba Ram Dass, the ex-Harvard-professor-turned-guru. Ram Dass is describing the talks he used to have with his brother, who was in a mental hospital.

> And my brother often said to me, "I don't know," he says, "I'm a lawyer, I'm a decent citizen, I've got a tie and a jacket, and I go to church, and I'm a good person and I read the Bible. Me they've got in a mental hospital; you, you walk barefoot, you've got a beard, you've got a funny name.... You, you're out free. How do you explain that?" And I say, "Well, I'll show you how." I said, "Do you think you're Christ? the Christ in pure consciousness?" He says, "Yes." I say, "Well I think I am too." And he looks at me and he says, "No, you don't understand." I say, "That's why they lock you up, you see. Because the minute you tell somebody else they're not Christ, they lock you up. The minute you say, 'I am and you're not,' then you gotta go."

Of course, it is not easy to put yourself instantly into Ram Dass's egalitarian frame of mind (or any other frame of mind, for that matter). When you are about to criticize the other person, you will often feel that you *are* something he isn't. That is why the techniques in this chapter can be so helpful. Each technique automatically tends to push you into the state of mind Ram Dass is talking about. You don't suddenly have to swing your head around; the techniques do it for you.

> *Democracy means not "I'm as good as you are," but "you're as good as I am."*
>
> —THEODORE PARKER

Sometimes you may find it also helps you get into the proper frame of mind for committing tolerable criticism if you *criticize yourself before criticizing the other person.* By doing this, you literally demonstate that you as well as the other person are prone to mistake and error, that is, you avoid implying "I am, and you're not." Of course if you only criticize yourself in token fashion before really laying into the other person, you won't have made your criticism much more tolerable.

All right, but sometimes you are going to be so steamed up that you won't have the calm or discipline needed to employ some of the techniques in this chapter (and you certainly won't feel like criticizing yourself first). What can you do? Perhaps the best approach is to try to hold off completely from any criticism until you are a bit cooler—the old "count to ten when you're mad" idea. A good rule of thumb to follow is: *If you can't image something positive or good about the other person, postpone your criticism.* This doesn't mean necessarily finding something good about what the other person *just* said or did (although that technique is certainly worthwhile and has already been discussed). It does mean being able to think of something favorable about the other person, *anything* he has done or said in the past that was nice or valuable. If you cannot feel or image anything good about that person, chances are you are in no proper frame of mind for committing tolerable criticism.

If you can't image anything positive, and you don't feel you can postpone your outburst, then as a last resort try putting together some combination of the following phrases:

"Look, I'm really upset right now."

"I need a chance to blow off some steam."

"Let me get this off my chest now."

"Please don't argue or interrupt me."

"Later I'll try to discuss it with you more rationally and calmly."

> *What is important here is not that men disagree, but that they become disagreeable about it.*
>
> —IRVING J. LEE

SUMMARY CHART: TECHNIQUES FOR COMMITTING TOLERABLE CRITICISM

Approaches	*Related Verbal Formulas*
1. Understand first, criticize later.	Use paraphrase as discussed in chapter 1.
2. Express as personal opinion not as "right" or "truth."	"In my opinion . . ."; "The way I see it is . . ."; "I feel that . . ."; "Sometimes"; "Maybe"; "Possibly."
3. Criticize the idea, opinion, or action—not the person.	
4. Criticize process as well as content.	
5. Be as specific as possible.	Avoid "never," "always," "everything," and similar words; instead, use "When you said . . ."; "Right now I feel . . ."; "In this specific instance. . . ."

6. Criticize one thing at a time.

7. Point out the negative consequences that follow from your critical observation.

Follow your critical observation with a "Therefore . . ." or a "So . . ." or an "As a result. . . ."

8. Make the criticism action oriented.
   A. State criticism as a problem.
   B. Suggest action alternatives.

"The problem is how to . . ."

9. Include some credits along with the criticism.

Use "and" phrases instead of "but" phrases.

10. Criticize yourself before criticizing the other person.

11. If you can't image something positive about the other person, postpone your criticism.

12. If you are so mad you can't do any of the above, then explain that you need a chance to blow off some steam and will discuss it more calmly later.

4 Making Credits Believable

There's no business like snow business!

CREDIT ABILITY GAPS

- In the 1930s Dale Carnegie wrote *How to Win Friends and Influence People.*
- Norman Vincent Peale's *The Power of Positive Thinking* has sold over three million copies.
- Eminent psychologist Carl Rogers finds the key to effective human relations is "unconditional positive regard."
- B. F. Skinner's extensive research clearly demonstrates that you can modify behavior through positive reinforcement.
- Positive "strokes" are at the heart of Eric Berne's now popular Transactional Analysis approach.

For fifty years and more, a good deal of research and writing in the field of psychology has trumpeted forth the potent, beneficial effects of compliments and credits. Clement Stone runs Success Rallies that draw crowds of ten thousand people and up. Humaneering, Inc., conducts several Positive Thinking Rallies every month for masses just as large. In almost every field of endeavor now, we are urged to apply the techniques of positive thinking (to ourselves as well as to others).

- Teachers are urged to think favorably about the ability of their students.
- Bosses are exhorted to give more recognition to their subordinates.
- Doctors are advised to give their patients confidence and hope, which seem to cure as well as any prescription.
- Salesmen are trained to think positively about making the sale.
- Parents are counseled to shower each other and their offspring with plenty of praise.

Some authorities recommend that eight out of ten comments to another person should be positive. How far most of us are from that mark!

This chapter, then, starts from the assumption that you are already convinced that giving praise or credit is something worthwhile doing, for its own sake as well as being an important way of making your criticism more tolerable. The intriguing issue is that considering all the evidence for and exhortations to give credits, why do so many of us still hand out far less than the suggested quota of positive comments? In discussing this issue with a number of people, I find the same two problems keep cropping up:

1. how to overcome the fear of saying too much
2. how to make a credit believable

The Fear of Saying Too Much

In a friendly or social setting, how the other person interprets our credit may not be very significant. But in more important, serious situations, we may worry a great deal about what the other person thinks we are really saying. Here is how one manager in a large consumer services organization expressed it:

> I know that handing out compliments is supposed to motivate people. What worries me, though, is that when I tell an employee he's done a good job on something, he goes off thinking he is all-around terrific. And

if I do that a couple of times, next thing I know, he'll be in my office asking why he hasn't gotten a raise—you know, for his "superb performance." The other thing I've found is that the guy will make darn sure that other people in the firm hear about how highly I think of him. One way or another, that's going to get back to my other subordinates. And then they get upset because they didn't get the same kind of praise, and they think they're doing just as good a job; or worse, they feel the first employee didn't really deserve the praise in the first place.

Now, this kind of concern exists not only between managers and subordinates, but it also creeps in between friends or family members.

> *Oh, I find it much easier to give a credit than a criticism. You don't have to worry so much about hurting the other person. Funny thing, though, most people seem to have trouble receiving my compliments. They get embarrassed and try to shrug it off, and I feel sort of awkward about the whole thing. I don't quite understand it, but it probably keeps me from handing out praise as much as I might.*
> —A SUBURBAN HOUSEWIFE

The Problem of Believability

Much of the crediting we give or receive occurs in the course of social pleasantries; whereas negative criticism is typically reserved for more serious, important occasions. Thus, to some degree, a positive comment may tend to seem trivial or superficial.

Also, we learn from experience (as well as from our parents) that compliments, not criticisms, are the way to ingratiate ourselves with others, the way to "get ahead." We are warned that others won't like being criticized. Thus, to some degree, a credit tends to be suspect, possibly conniving, potentially devious.

So, it can be difficult to distinguish a genuine, heartfelt credit from its superficial or suspect brethren. We worry that the other person will not really believe our credit, not take it seriously. And, in fact, the other person often does slough off our credit—which can make us feel uncomfortable and less inclined to hand out credits in the future.

The Basic Approach

The next three sections essentially discuss ways to limit and define more precisely what you are crediting. This general approach helps you differentiate your serious credit from the more superficial, social kind of small talk (which is typically much more general). And the specificity of the credit helps emphasize the genuine nature of what you are saying; the credit is less likely to be perceived as something manufactured, made up for the purposes of insincere flattery. Fortuitously, at the same time that you are enhancing the believability of your credit by being precise, you are also minimizing the chances that the other person will hear more in your credit than you wished to convey.

There are two key parts to this basic approach:

1. finding something genuine to credit
2. finding appropriate words to deliver the credit

Each of these two key parts will be treated in turn in the next sections of this chapter.

> *An intelligent man finds something*
> *ridiculous in almost everything, a*
> *wise man in hardly anything.*
>
> —GERMAN PROVERB

PUSHING FOR POSITIVES

Clearly, if you haven't found something you feel worthy of a credit, then no matter what you say, the chances are your credit won't sound very believable. But we are not generally in the habit of pushing ourselves to find something specific to like in what another person says or does. There may be several explanations for this. Some psychologists claim we are merely doing unto others what we do to ourselves. That is, we are in the habit of putting ourselves down much of the time. And it is all too easy just to extend that habit and put others down as well. Another theory is that our basic drives for safety and security lead us to focus primarily on the potential problems or pitfalls of any idea or action. A third possibility is that we simply take a lot of good things for granted because they are expected. For instance, on the job, a boss *expects* his subordinates to be competent, to do good work, no matter how rare such competence may actually be. Thus, a good job brings no special praise from the boss, any more than the receipt of the weekly paycheck brings forth a special thank-you from the subordinate. When our expectations are met, we tend to react neutrally. Only when our expectations are exceeded do lights flash and bells ring for us.

Whatever the explanation, the point is that often we will not see the positives in what another person says or does unless we consciously push ourselves to look for them. The fascinating thing is that it turns out that almost any idea or thought or action does have something useful and worthwhile in it.

Just to prove the point, I developed the most absurd proposition I could think of for discussion in a seminar group. The proposition I presented was this:

> Resolved that the United States should immediately turn over all its nuclear and other armaments to the Soviet Union for safekeeping.

I asked the group, "How many people feel this is a good idea?" No one felt it was. I then asked the seminar to split up into small groups, and I challenged each group to come up with as many "positives" about the proposition as they could in fifteen minutes. At first the participants felt this was a ludicrous assignment. There was much joking and sarcastic muttering within the little subgroups. Slowly (if reluctantly) the groups settled down to the task.

Right now, see if *you* can come up with a couple of things that might be useful or worthwhile in that same, seemingly absurd proposition:

1. _____
2. _____

Really, go ahead and try. Your effort will make the following discussion much more meaningful.

At the end of the fifteen-minute period, the small groups were rather astounded at the lists they had compiled. Some of the positives they came up with are listed below:

1. eliminates the storage problem
2. reduces chances of accidental mishaps
3. frees up plants for domestic production
4. could reduce taxes
5. might create better rapport with other nations
6. reduces probability of nuclear war
7. might increase level of trust and cooperation between U.S. and Russia
8. would help conserve oil and other forms of energy
9. would provide increased space for circuses
10. would generate a lot of business for U.S. transport companies, who would end up transferring the materials

All in all, the seminar came up with some thirty positives. At this point one of the participants acidly commented, "Okay, but I still don't think it's a good idea." "That's not the point," chorused several others. They went on to say that it was surprising how different the proposition now looked. Certainly they had not become ardent supporters of the idea. But at the very least, they had become much clearer about just what such an idea might really mean; and *not everything* about the idea was ridiculous. Some of the group members even felt quite seriously that some of the positives were worthy of further exploration, albeit in a somewhat less extreme context.

Pushing for positives does not guarantee in any way that you will change your mind about a particular idea. But you will increase your understanding of what the idea involves; and you are likely to come up with some new ways of looking at or thinking about the problem; you may even come up with some new alternatives or thoughts for action. At a minimum, pushing for positives does guarantee that the person suggesting the idea will not feel like an idiot, and therefore he may have less of a desire to prove you the idiot for totally rejecting his idea.

It does require effort to find genuine positives, yet the more you learn to push for positives, the fewer ideas you will find that have nothing positive about them. There are no guaranteed gambits for finding positives, but in the next section are a few approaches that may help.

> *It is a very sad thing nowadays there is so little useless information.*
>
> —OSCAR WILDE

> *I am so confident that nearly every proposition is true in the manner intended by the speaker, that I never contradict.*
>
> —A. B. JOHNSON

Don't Take What the Other Person Says Too Literally

Ideas or comments are rarely verbalized in exact and precise form, although often they may sound as if they are. You don't have to take the thought word for word as it is expressed. Remember from chapter 1 that people often don't really know what they think until they see what they say, and even then they may not be as sure as they sound.

DON'T REACT TO THE IDEA AS AN INVIOLABLE WHOLE

Take the "arms to Russia" idea as an example. Suppose you separate the idea of turning over arms to someone from the idea that the "someone" should be Russia. Certainly the strategy of turning arms over to a neutral party is far from silly. The idea has been suggested a number of times by various international diplomats and has even been tried out in a limited way.

Similarly, the idea of turning over something military can be separated from the idea that the something need be physical munitions or armaments. In fact, the idea of trading military *knowledge* has been seriously considered by the Pentagon, that is, the notion that giving the enemy certain information can relieve secret fears and thus create a more workable balance of power.

Notice how the tenor of the proposition quickly changes if you simply ignore the italicized words—*"immediately* turn over *all* its nuclear and other armaments." For many years now, there have been actual disarmament talks about the possibilities of phasing out certain weapons over a *period of time.* Perhaps there are *some* armaments that it would make sense to share with the Soviets.

DON'T CONSIDER THE IDEA TO BE NECESSARILY COMPLETE

In a few sentences or even paragraphs it is almost impossible to present the full-blown detail of an idea. Nonetheless, a statement of an idea often does sound complete unto itself, even though upon questioning the speaker would quickly admit that there is more to the idea than what he just said. Thus, turning over certain arms to Russia might make good sense if in turn Russia turned over certain arms to the U.S. Or the shipment of arms might work if it were followed up by some sort of security check.

Consider the Process as Well as the Content

The last chapter talked about criticizing "process" as well as content, because often the process is what is really upsetting. Conversely, you can also look to the process to find something you like about what the other person is saying or doing. For instance, you may not like the idea of shipping arms (any arms) to Russia (or anyone else), but you could still find it meritorious that the other person is thinking about ways to diminish the level of hostility between the two countries. In other words, you may find a positive in what the other person is trying to do, even though you disagree with the specific proposal or opinion.

In essence, *any idea or action is only an approximation.* If you are able to "hear" the idea as only such an approximation, then you open up many avenues for positive reaction, and you can encourage building upon a part of the idea that you find interesting or worthwhile.

Even if you don't find anything directly positive about either the process or content of the other person's thought, there may still be something useful in what he says. For example, the other person's comment or action may cause you to think about a new aspect of the problem or situation, you may get a new idea, or you may simply confirm further your original thinking. But any one or all of these things have worth. They can be the focus of your credit. (For more on how what the other person says can be helpful or useful even if you don't accept or agree with it, see pages 107–118.)

Finding something worthwhile in what the other person says isn't always easy. You may have to overlook part of what was said, not interpret the statement too literally, use your own imagination or ingenuity to spark off of what was actually said. And there are many kinds of usefulness. But the positives are there, if only you are able to recognize them.

> *I made it a rule to forbear all direct*
> *contradiction to the sentiments of*
> *others. . . . When another asserted*
> *something that I thought an error, I*
> *deny'd myself the pleasure of*
> *contradicting him abruptly, and of*
> *showing immediately some absurdity*
> *in his proposition; and in answering I*
> *began by observing that in certain*
> *cases or circumstances his opinion*
> *would be right.*
>
> —BENJAMIN FRANKLIN

TECHNIQUES FOR EXPRESSING CREDITS

> *I guess I probably don't give out*
> *enough praise. I've read a lot about*
> *how important it is to provide positive*
> *reinforcement and all that stuff, but it*
> *just seems hard to do. Even when*
> *somebody really has done a bang-up*
> *job, it seems like I just don't know*
> *quite what to say.*
> —A CORPORATE MANAGER

Even when you have found something genuine to credit, even when you feel very much like giving a credit, you may still worry about how to express your credit believably or about how to say no more than you mean. In short, you need some verbal approaches. As it turns out, most of the verbal approaches for making a credit believable are quite similar to those for making your criticism more tolerable. So this section examines each of the techniques for committing tolerable criticism to see how it might apply in making your credits more believable.

Understand First, Credit Later

No doubt the other person would rather hear a credit than a criticism, with or without understanding. A credit that does not demonstrate some degree of understanding, however, is very likely to be perceived as a social nicety or a form of insincere flattery. After all, if you don't know what you are talking about, then it is certainly difficult for the other person to put much stock in what you are saying, no matter how pleasant the sound.

Express Credit as Opinion, Not as "Right" or "Truth"

The merit of this technique for crediting may not be quite as obvious as the need for understanding what you are crediting. Wouldn't proclaiming a credit as a fact or the truth be highly desirable to the other person? Wouldn't that person like his credit certified by some official seal as 99 and 94/100 percent pure, objective truth? (Incidentally, your knowing what you are talking about is at least a small step in this direction.)

The odds are, however, that, deep down, the other person realizes there can be no such guaranteed seal of approval. Even if he feels there may be such an official source, he probably doesn't think it is you. There is also a little "catch-22" in all this as well; if the other person allows himself to view you as a fountainhead of truth, then your criticism as well as your credits must be accepted as hard fact.

Anyway, underneath it all, the other person probably feels there can be some difference of opinion about what he has said or done. So you make it difficult for that other person to accept your credit when you state it too strongly as "the way it is." If any criticism is always just an opinion, then so is any credit. Better to preface your credit with one of the personalizing phrases suggested in chapter 3:

"In my opinion . . ."

"The way I see it is . . ."

"I feel that . . ."

"I think that . . ."

Or you can use one of these phrases, which are more positive but which still indicate that the judgment is yours:

"I like (or appreciate) . . ."

"I'm pleased that . . ."

"I'm proud of you for . . ."

Crediting Ideas, Opinions, or Actions Versus Crediting the Person

Each of the examples below shows two alternative ways of expressing a particular credit:

1A. "I think that meal we just had was really great."

1B. "I think you really are a great cook."

2A. "In this presentation it seems to me you certainly have thought through the problem carefully."

2B. "It seems to me you have that ability to think things through carefully."

The left-hand ("A") credits refer primarily to what the other person has said or done. They avoid the implication that the other person *always* does a particular thing or that he *is* a particular way. While we can enjoy being told that we are marvelous, most of us realize we are not always brilliant or careful or successful or whatever. In fact many of us like to feel we are (or can be) a few different things at various times. On occasion we are very thorough, and sometimes we aren't or don't need to be; sometimes we can cook up a storm, and sometimes the food doesn't turn out so well (or we are great with meats and not so good with pastry). Thus, crediting ideas, opinions, or actions may make the praise more believable, easier to accept. Such credits may also minimize the dangers of the other person developing a swelled head, attributing more to the credit than you really mean.

The right-hand ("B") credits praise some general trait of the other person, something the other person *is*. In one sense, then, they are more of a credit, because the credit is not restricted to a particular thing. The argument for making the right-hand type of credit is that it may allow the other person to feel that his talents can extend to other actions or ideas; therefore, this type of credit may provide more encouragement.

Well, the authorities seem to disagree about which type of credit is the most effective. So take your choice of which type of credit you prefer to give. Personally, I lean toward giving (and receiving) the left-hand type of credit, if only because it is somewhat more specific, an important consideration to be discussed next.

Be Specific

Being specific is one of the most crucial techniques for making credits believable. At the same time, the more specific you are, the less likely you are to be heard as saying more than you mean. Moreover, the really credit-worthy part of what was said or done may be easier to find in a specific detail than in the overall idea or action.

Now, there is nothing wrong in starting off your credit with a somewhat general statement that conveys the positive nature of your credit. But see how much is added by a more specific follow-up. For example:

General Credit	*More Specific Credit*
"I think that meal we just had was really great."	"I especially enjoyed that sauce on the meat."

Somehow, the mention of a specific detail suggests that you were really paying attention and are not just tossing off a social nicety.

As with criticism, all-inclusive words such as "never," "every time," or "completely" do not make for specificity. The other person may warm to the personal loyalty of your saying, "You *always* cook such great meals," but the credit just doesn't come across as highly believable. Even Julia Child occasionally burns something.

Crediting One Thing at a Time

This technique is not nearly as important for crediting as it is for criticism. Most of us seem to have a much greater tolerance for absorbing credits than for criticisms. Of course, you can go to an extreme and credit so many things that the other person loses track, or, worse, begins to feel you aren't being genuine.

Point Out the Positive Effects

This way of being specific really does enhance the value and believability of a credit. For example:

> "It was really important that you thought through this problem carefully because there are a lot of bucks riding on the decision we're going to make"

> or

> ". . . because my boss has been on my back to get this situation cleared up"

> or

> ". . . because now I really understand the alternatives and won't look silly when the subject comes up at our next planning meeting"

Describing the impact of the good thing the other person has said or done serves as proof that it really was "good." Mentioning the positive effects helps establish that you aren't just saying something nice in order to butter up the other person or just trying to make him feel good.

Don't Taint Your Credit with a Criticism

The previous chapter suggested tempering your criticism with credits. In parallel fashion, it might seem reasonable to include a criticism or two along with your credit—perhaps something like this:

> "Although there were a couple of awkward places and there is one point I wish you had included, in general it seems to me you certainly have thought through the problem carefully."

Do you see how the other person may hear this as a criticism made more tolerable by the presence of a credit, instead of hearing it as a credit made more believable through the presence of a criticism?

As it happens, criticism and credits are not completely symmetrical opposites. Most of us find it easier to detect what we don't like than to single out what we like. Perhaps this is because many of us worry more about problems that still exist than rejoice in solutions already found; we brood over our failures or lacks more than we take cheer from our successes. Of course, if you are the extreme optimist who finds most things terrific, then perhaps you should spice your credits with a criticism every now and then. Otherwise your credits risk coming off as not very believable. But for most of us, leaving a credit untainted by a criticism is much the preferable route.

> *An optimist thinks this is the best of all possible worlds.*
> *A pessimist is afraid it is.*

PUTTING IT ALL TOGETHER

Below is a summary chart of the various techniques for crediting, adapted from the similar list for criticizing. The chart also provides a comment about the importance or relevance of each technique.

SUMMARY CHART: TECHNIQUES FOR MAKING CREDITS BELIEVABLE

Technique	*Comment*
1. Understand first, credit later.	very basic
2. Express credit as opinion, not as "right" or "truth."	useful
3. Credit the idea, opinion, or action—not the person.	debatable—personally I lean toward using it
4. Be specific.	very effective
5. Credit one thing at a time.	useful, but not crucial
6. Point out the positive effects.	very effective

7. Don't taint the credit with a criticism.	useful much of the time
8. Make the credit action-oriented.	not relevant (not discussed in chapter but included here because the technique was listed in the chapter on criticism)—presumably a credit does not create a problem nor call for action

Notice that the summary-chart comments describe the effectiveness of the various techniques for dealing with the problem of saying too much (as well as the problem of believability)—except in the case of technique #7. It is possible to argue that tainting your credit with a criticism will keep the other person from feeling he is *too* marvelous; the risk, of course, is that by so doing, the other person won't feel marvelous at all.

Now, here are a few examples that show how some of the various crediting techniques can work together in what you say. The words in parentheses underneath some of the lines indicate which technique is being used in that part of the credit.

1. Wife talking to her husband about an incident with their son Michael:

    "Well, in my opinion, you handled that problem
        (*personal opinion*)

    with Mike really well. I mean you held your temper,
    (*general credit—of action*)   (*more specific credit*)

    and you got *him* to come up with some of his own ideas
        (*another more specific credit*)

    about what to do. And I think this way, he's really
    likely to do something about it."
        (*statement of effect*)

2. Boss speaking to a subordinate:

"I just wanted to say that I think you've put in an
                    (*personal opinion*)

awful lot of extra effort recently, and I particularly
            (*general credit—of action*)

appreciate your willingness to stay late this week.
                    (*more specific credit*)

As a result, you know, we're going to be able to get
this project out to the customer on schedule. Remember,
            (*statement of effect*)

this guy could generate a lot of business for us."
                    (*additional effect*)

3. One manager talking to another manager in a group meeting:

"Now, as I understand it, you're suggesting that we hire
back temporarily one of our recently retired workers,
                    (*stating understanding*)

right? [pauses to get confirmation—which he does] And
I think that's a terrific idea; I especially like the
                    (*general credit*)

idea of hiring someone who is already familiar with our way
                            (*more specific credit*)

of doing things, because you know how our competition has
been capitalizing on our quality problems. One thing,
            (*statement of effect*)

though, this will mean something else for Karl to worry
                    (*a bit of criticism*)

about. I'd really like to find a way to avoid this,
            (*criticism stated as a problem to be solved*)

because he is terrifically overloaded right now."

Whether or not you adopt all the approaches of this chapter,
at least you should realize more clearly how praising can pose as

much of a problem as criticizing. You probably recognized long ago that it is worth worrying about how you deliver a criticism. You may have felt, however, that praise is somehow always welcome, no matter the form. Certainly praise is usually more welcome than criticism, no matter the form. But the point is that it can take as much effort to make a credit believable as it does to make a criticism tolerable. Using the verbal techniques of this chapter can help ensure that your credit is good almost anywhere.

> *In his private heart, no man much respects himself.*
>
> —MARK TWAIN

BONUS SECTION—
RECEIVING CREDITS GRACEFULLY

There is a problem not only in giving a credit but also in getting one. How curious! Receiving a credit is good news, something that you usually find pleasant, and yet quite often you may feel awkward about what to say in response. If the credit is couched in the terms suggested in the previous part of this chapter, you may find it easier to respond, but still some difficulties remain. Here's the bind:

- If you believe you deserve (or have deserved) the credit, then to say so sounds immodest—and modesty, in our culture, has been a highly prized virtue
- If you don't believe the credit is merited, then to agree with the credit is dishonest.

This bind can make it hard for you to accept a credit, regardless of whether the credit is for a good job or a pretty dress. To slough off a credit, you may resort to one or more of these common methods:

1. disagree with it or deny it, for example, "Oh, I don't know" or "I'm not sure about that"

2. make light (or a joke) of it, for example, "Oh, that was nothing" or "You mean that old thing?"

3. explain it away, for example, "I was just lucky" or "It was just an accident"

4. return a token compliment in exchange; for example, "I admire your work too" or "Your dress is pretty also" (which tends to make the tenor of the whole conversation one of social niceties)

5. say nothing and give a shrug of the shoulders, letting the credit "roll off"

Responding to a credit by any one (or all) of these approaches just transfers the bind back to the other person:

- If the other person feels he is giving you a genuine credit, then your nonacceptance implies that he was in error or has poor judgment.
- If the other person knows that his credit was just a social nicety or an attempt to butter you up, then your nonacceptance implies that his insincerity has been found out.

At best the other person will interpret your denial of his credit as false modesty or perhaps as fishing for more of a credit. (Ever notice how some people just don't seem to hear a credit the first time you give it, and you have to repeat it for them?)

So what started out as a simple attempt to give you a credit may end up with both you and the other person feeling in a bind and quite uncomfortable about the whole matter. Surely this is not a state of affairs that will encourage the other person to give you more credits in the future.

One way to stop some of the unnecessary nonsense is for you simply to *accept the credit* in the first place, accept it for exactly what it is: just another person's opinion, and a pleasant one at that. You don't have to agree with the credit; you are not necessarily what the credit says you are. One of these phrases may suffice:

"Thank you!" (That's certainly simple enough, isn't it?)

"It's nice of you to say that."

At least this way you indicate that you heard the compliment and have not rejected it. If you want to go a bit further, the secret is to talk about your good feeling at being credited. For example:

"I like to hear that." (or "I appreciate knowing that.")

"That makes me feel good."

"I'm happy you feel that way."

These phrases allow you to sound pleased at receiving the credit; you do not slough off the credit; yet you avoid directly agreeing (or disagreeing) with the substance of the credit.

Well, try out these few types of reactions, and suddenly you may find that you are much more credit-worthy!

> *He who refuses praise the first time*
> *that it is offered does so because he*
> *would hear it a second time.*
> —DUC DE LA ROCHEFOUCAULD

5 Help!

Most people accept good advice—if it doesn't interfere with their plans.
—PAUL HARWITZ

Advice is seldom welcome, and those who want it the most always like it the least.
—LORD CHESTERFIELD

No one can help you but yourself. Nonsense! Of course it's wonderful to see men and women act with a sense of self-reliance, but it's something else to posit that everyone should be or is or even can be completely self-sufficient. At one point or another we all have occasion to need or want help from another person. The problem is that *most of the time we ask for the wrong kind of help and we get it.*

This chapter deals with how to go about getting help, not how to give it. Much has been written about the latter, and very little about the former. Perhaps that's because it is more blessed to give than to receive. Or maybe it's just easier to give help than to receive it.

The full line of help you can get includes a large variety of shapes and sizes. Getting help can mean

- receiving assistance with a task, that is, the other person literally performs a part of the work, say, of moving furniture, shoveling snow, writing a report, preparing a budget or planning a trip; sometimes the work may be formally assigned or delegated to a subordinate or spouse, and so on;
- engaging in formal therapy with a professional psychologist or psychiatrist;
- getting advice or counsel about a problem or situation in the home or on the job.

The last kind of help is the focal point for this chapter. You have a problem or situation that requires a decision or some action. For instance, you want to ask your boss for a raise and don't quite know how to go about it, or you aren't sure where to take your vacation, or you are trying to decide which subordinate to promote, or you would like to cut down your expenses, or your daughter is having math problems at school. The issue may be emotionally heavy or just important and complicated, but you feel it would be useful to get some help from your spouse or a friend or a co-worker. You want the other person to advise or counsel you about how to handle the situation, but you do not expect that other person actually to handle the situation *for* you.

Now, you'll find it easier to follow this chapter if you have one of your own specific situations in mind—a situation where you felt the need for getting advice. So take a minute and jot down your brief answers to the questions that follow.

Questions on Help—to Clarify Your Own Experience

1. When did you most recently ask someone for advice or help?
   ☐ today   ☐ last month
   ☐ yesterday   ☐ over six months ago
   ☐ last week   ☐ last year

2. To get your example clearly in mind, describe in a sentence what help you asked for in this most recent case.

   _____

   _____

3. What kind of help did you really want most? (not necessarily what you asked for or what you actually received)

☐ support (for your position)
☐ opinion
☐ information
☐ decision
☐ an answer

☐ an idea or two
☐ clarification of your own thoughts
☐ an alternative
☐ an evaluation
☐ observations or insights

something else _____

4. Did you get most of what you really wanted?
☐ yes
☐ no

5. In hindsight, what did you get that was most *useful* (regardless of whether or not it was something you thought you wanted originally)?

☐ support (for your position)
☐ opinion
☐ information
☐ decision
☐ an answer

☐ an idea or two
☐ clarification of your own thoughts
☐ an alternative
☐ an evaluation
☐ observations or insights

something else _____

The responses of other people to these same questions will be discussed at various points in this chapter. In the meantime, if you did not answer the questions, why not go back and do so. That way you'll be able to compare your own experience with that of the others.

The responses to question #1 clearly indicate that most people ask for advice or counsel very frequently. Few respondents had to look any further back than "yesterday" to find an instance of asking for advice.

The answers to question #2 confirm the broad range of issues on which people seek advice. For example:

- A teacher asks a colleague about a low mark she may have to give one of her students.
- A manager asks a subordinate to help him think through the purchase of a new piece of equipment.
- A father asks his daughter for help in understanding what he did to make her mother so upset.
- A doctor calls up another doctor to discuss a complicated diagnosis.

Question #3 asked about the kind of advice that was most wanted. In brief, the responses indicated that different people ask for different kinds of advice at different times. Getting each type of advice poses its own set of problems and calls for a unique set of verbal approaches, which is what the rest of this chapter is all about.

> *Everybody is ignorant, only on different subjects.*
> —WILL ROGERS

YOU'RE ASKING FOR IT
(Categories of Counsel)

> *Any man can prove he has good judgment by saying you have.*
> —LAURENCE J. PETER

Suing for Moral Support

The answers to question #3, above, indicate that what a lot of people want when they ask for help is moral support or encouragement—when they are really honest about what they want. They would like to know that what they are planning to do (or have done) is right or good or appropriate, that is, obtain support for their own position. As C. C. Colton put it, "We ask advice, but we mean approbation."

In some ways, however, wanting this kind of help represents a bit of the impossible dream. Basically what we are asking for is that the other person give us his honest opinion, but simultaneously we are asking him to agree with us. Now, if that other person honestly does agree with us, how will we know that, since we also asked him to agree with us? If the other person honestly doesn't agree with us, he has one of two equally unfortunate choices: He may tell us his honest opinion, in which case we don't get the support we wanted; or he may ignore his own opinion and tell us what we want to hear. But if we sense that the other person isn't giving us his true opinion, then his agreement won't provide much moral support anyway.

The way many of us deal with this dilemma is to ask directly for the other person's opinion and then subtly, indirectly suggest that it is important for him to agree with our position. If that doesn't work, we may continue by asserting our position very strongly, by logically arguing for the correctness of our view, or by modifying our description of the situation so that our position meets the objections of our helper. And when all else fails, we may resort to the time-tested approach of seeking another opinion . . . and another opinion . . . and another opinion until we find someone willing to say that he sees it our way.

Sometimes we can fool ourselves with these approaches, convince ourselves that we are really getting the other person's true position. More often, we find that winning the game of approbation provides a hollow victory. It's hard to fool ourselves into thinking we didn't stack the deck. And somehow the approbation game gets addicting; we never seem to win enough of it.

A better approach may be for us to realize that our desire for moral support really involves two different elements: a desire for emotional warmth or sympathy and a desire for confirmation of our opinion or position. So far as warmth and sympathy are concerned, there is no reason why we cannot state that desire straight out with phrases like these:

"I'm really worried about this thing, and I need a sympathetic ear."

"I guess I need some TLC." (tender, loving care)

(For more about stating feelings, see chapter 8.) When our need for this part of moral support is very strong, we had probably better try to get it. If we don't, it is unlikely that we will be able to move on to any other part of the problem; we will certainly find it difficult to pay attention to any other kinds of advice our helper might offer.

So far as our desire for confirmation is concerned, perhaps the best we can do is simply to express it as a wish or a hope (rather than indirectly demanding it). For example:

"I must admit, I hope you're going to agree with me on this, but I guess I can accept it if you don't."

"It sure would be nice if you came out the same way as I do on this, but it won't help me much if I don't get your honest opinion."

At least this way the game is aboveboard. At least this way, if we get approbation, the odds are somewhat higher that we will find it truly helpful.

When I want your opinion, I'll give it to you.

—LAURENCE J. PETER

Rufus Mile's Law

Where you stand depends on where you sit!

Asking for Answers

Sometimes when we ask for advice, what we want is for the other person to give us the answer or to make the decision for us. Even when we ask for an "opinion" or an "evaluation," we may still really want an answer or a decision. We may naturally seek this kind of advice when we consult a supposedly professional expert such as a doctor or a lawyer or, say, a computer specialist. But often we also seek the same kind of help from a colleague or a friend. It may be that we feel unknowledgeable about the subject matter of our problem or that we have not found an acceptable answer or that we are torn between several different alternatives for action.

Usually we won't have much trouble getting this kind of assist-ance. Asking for this kind of help typically flatters the other person; it implies that he is intelligent or knowledgeable and that he has worth as a person. Often the other person will try like crazy to give us an answer or decision (even if he doesn't really have one).

The basic problem with this kind of advice is that the other person isn't us. No one else is ever exactly in the same position as we are. No one has quite the same values as we do, and such value choices underlie almost every decision; for example, the balance between such factors as these:

- convenience versus cost
- success versus security
- the future versus the present

Usually such values are not formally discussed, even between close friends. So when we hear the other person's answer or recommended decision, we may not have a clear idea of what value choices were made; and we quite properly suspect that the other person's way of juggling values may not correspond to our own. Perhaps this is why we are often not sure what to do with the answers or decisions another person offers us; we are somehow not completely willing to adopt them. Around the year 20 B.C. Dionysius of Halicarnassus put it this way, "All men judge the acts of others by what they would have done themselves."

Of course, we can ask each one of a number of different people for their answers and then tally up the votes or take an opinion poll. After all, that's the democratic way! Such tac-tics may work (or be the only alternative) for settling national policy matters in Washington, D.C., but with a more personal matter such an approach tends just to generate more confu-sion.

The real joker is that if any other person were truly in the same position as we and completely shared our values, that person simply would be as confused or undecided as we are. There just don't seem to be any effective verbal gambits for getting out of these difficulties. Perhaps the moral is that *if you're looking for other people to give you answers and decisions, don't!*

> We give advice, but we cannot give conduct.
>
> —*attributed to* DUC DE LA ROCHEFOUCAULD and to BENJAMIN FRANKLIN

Eye-Opening Help

Asking for approbation is chancy at best. Expecting the other person to provide a definitive solution is not very realistic. What kind of advice or counsel is left? It's what might be called "eye-opening" advice, and it includes these four "I's":

- *i*deas, that is, new possibilities or additional alternatives
- *i*nformation, that is, new pieces of data or different ways of organizing the information you have
- *i*nstruction—on how to think through or analyze the problem or situation
- *i*nsights—that point out flaws in your logic, that clarify a muddy part of the situation, that shift your perspective, that redefine the problem

Eye-opening help capitalizes on the fact that the other person isn't you, instead of fighting it. Precisely because the other person isn't you, she is likely to say something new about your problem, something that is new for you, that you hadn't known or thought about before.

Question #3 (back on page 96) asked about the kind of advice that was most wanted. Few people singled out one of the eye-openers. Yet their answers to question #5 confirmed that *eye-openers are often the most helpful part of whatever advice you get.* Here in some detail is one of the situations that was reported (more briefly) on the questionnaire.

> BILL—a manager in the market research department of the Sheridan Company

SAM—one of Bill's subordinates

FRED—a manager in the sales department and a friend of both Bill and Sam

Bill was trying to decide whether or not to assign a very important research project to Sam. Though Sam was bright enough, his work in the past had been uneven. On the other hand, Bill was worried that if he gave the project to someone else, Sam might be very upset. Bill explained the situation to Fred and asked his advice about what to do.

In bits and pieces during the discussion, Fred commented that he felt Sam was on a real psychological upswing now that his (Sam's) divorce had finally come through.

Afterward, in describing this discussion, Bill said, "I guess what I wanted was for Fred to make the decision for me, although I really knew he probably couldn't do that. What I really got from Fred that was helpful was a new piece of information and a related insight, because I hadn't known about Sam's divorce situation."

In other words, Bill had suddenly realized that some of the ups and downs in Sam's previous work might have been caused by the ups and downs of the divorce proceedings. Bill also learned that currently Sam might be in one of his more productive moods.

Notice that an eye-opener doesn't necessarily solve your problem. For instance, in the case above, Bill could have decided to give Sam the project because he felt that Sam's better frame of mind would assure a good job. Or Bill could have decided that because of Sam's good mood, Sam would better tolerate the assignment of the project to someone else.

Notice that eye-openers don't necessarily make your problem any easier (although sometimes they can). Learning about a new factor to consider or an additional alternative to analyze can make a situation seem more complex than it was before. Eye-openers often provide more questions than answers. But eye-openers are likely ultimately to help you deal more effectively with your problem, make a better decision, take a more appropriate action.

The price you pay for getting eye-openers is that you may have to exert some additional effort to incorporate them into your thinking. When someone just tells you whether he agrees with you or not or just indicates his preference for one of the alternatives you propose, then all you have to do is simply accept his opinion, reject it, or disregard it. When ideas, information, instruction, or insights are what you get, your job isn't so simple. You have to play around with a new fact or idea to see how it fits in with the rest of your thinking. The one new tidbit may trigger off additional areas for analysis or further facts to be gathered. In short, you have to decide what to do with an eye-opener and then do it.

You have to work to make eye-openers helpful once you get them and you have to work just as hard to get them in the first place. A simple opinion or evaluation is easy to come by. Anyone can offer a yes-or-no reaction on the most complex of issues. But coming up with new information or new possibilities often requires real thought, effort, and time. Moreover, people are not necessarily experienced in proffering the eye-opener kind of help —at least in part because they are not very often asked for it. As a result, many people also may not fully understand how the eye-opening part of their advice can truly be helpful to you.

ENCOURAGING EYE-OPENERS

If you want to get eye-openers, you have to make that especially clear in the way you ask for help, if only because so many requests for advice are for something else, namely moral support or definitive answers. But the way you react to what your helper says is also an important part of encouraging eye-openers, if only because the other person isn't used to providing this kind of help and may not realize its real value.

What follows is a series of verbal techniques that covers both asking more clearly for eye-openers and reacting appropriately to what your helper offers you. Near the end of this chapter is a sample dialogue that illustrates the techniques in actual use. You may find it helpful to refer to that dialogue from time to time as you read along through the various techniques.

Ask Straight Out for Eye-Openers

Don't ask the other person in a general way for "help" or "advice," because what you will tend to get is approbation or a quick opinion. If you're playing the game of help for eye-openers, then you need to explain the rules; otherwise you can hardly expect the other person to play the game, and you're the one that's dealing.

Even expressions like these may not fully clarify what you are looking for:

- "I'd like to get your *opinion.*"
- "I think your *perspective* would be very helpful."
- "Could you give me your *reactions* on this problem?"

Certainly the other person's opinion, perspective, or reactions may well contain some eye-openers. But by stressing these words you may create a false emphasis, an emphasis on the conclusion reached by the other person rather than on new input to help you reach your own conclusion. And remember that the other person is predisposed toward providing the "yes," "no," "I like this alternative" kind of help anyway.

Better to ask specifically for ideas, information, instruction, or insight, although again, even these words may still be heard by the other person as a request for a cursory opinion or evaluation. Adding one little extra word, however, can greatly increase the odds of getting the eye-openers you want. The key word to add is *new* or something equivalent. For example:

"What I'm really looking for are some *new* ideas on this."

"My feeling is that you may have some *new* information about this situation that I don't have."

"I hope you may see something I'm overlooking."

You may also want to take a moment and specifically explain that you are not looking for agreement with your position, that you do not expect the other person to come up with the definitive solution or answer, that you are more interested in the way he thinks about the situation than the particular conclusion he arrives at.

Don't Fill in Too Much Detail Too Soon

If you try to tell the other person everything he "ought" to know about the situation, you risk overloading him; and when people get overloaded they often feel uncomfortable, stop thinking clearly, or freeze up. Remember that it has probably taken you a long time to assemble all you know about a particular situation or problem. You can expect to transfer only a small part of what you know, only a rough feel for the situation. Moreover, you may not have realized that once your helper knows everything you do about the situation, you may have neatly biased him so that he will find it difficult to see anything new for you. Some lack of knowledge often allows another person to come up with ideas and options you have overlooked or perhaps prematurely rejected.

Listen to the Conclusions Anyway

Whether or not you ask for conclusions or definitive answers, you'll probably get them. You'll probably get a strong opinion or recommendation even if you specifically say you don't want one. So when the other person's conclusions start showing (which often occurs very early on), you might as well sit back and let her get all of them out. If you don't do this, you'll have trouble getting anything else.

If you don't prove you have heard the other person's suggestion or recommendation, you're likely to hear it again and again until you do prove you have heard it (or until the other person collapses from exhaustion). The paraphrase technique discussed back in chapter 1 will help you prove that you've heard. In fact, your paraphrasing by itself may even cause the other person to pop out a new idea or two for you as she goes about clarifying what she means (because your first attempt at restating her position won't be quite right).

*People are usually more firmly
convinced that their opinions are
precious than that they are true.*
——GEORGE SANTAYANA

Stifle Your Reaction

- "It's clear that what you have to do is . . ."
- "The only proper way to go is . . ."

These are the kinds of phrases that may accompany the other person's conclusions. Such phrases imply that right or truth is in the other person's vest pocket or are at least hovering nearby. Your reaction may quite naturally be, "Poppycock." Obviously if you voice this feeling, at best you will end up in an argument, and at worst you risk losing the cooperation of your helper.

One thing you can do is to recognize that whatever the other person says, it is only an *opinion,* because that is all any statement can really be. You may want mentally to tack on these words to what the other person says: ". . . in her opinion."

Now, even if the other person makes it clear he is only expressing a personal opinion, even if the other person doesn't make a recommendation but just expresses a new idea or possible alternative, you are still likely to have a reaction, be it a sigh of relief, a cry of disbelief, or something in between. Unless you are a consummate actor, your own point of view will show through. And that's all right as long as you don't react too strongly one way or the other. A strong reaction either way will cost you some eye-opening help, because the other person will respond to your reaction rather than continuing to think about the problem you want his ideas on.

Here are a few phrases you can use to help stifle your reaction:

"That's interesting."

"I'd not thought about it quite that way."

Essentially, these are cop-out phrases, that is, they don't say too much of anything, but they can be positive-enough sounding so that they don't cut off the flow of conversation. At least such a phrase gives you something to say.

You may find it harder to stifle your reaction if what the other person says includes some explicit or implicit slurs on you (or your spouse or dog).

- "I don't see how any reasonable person could do . . ."
- "You have to be out of your head to consider . . ."

Rather than defending yourself, try asking for more details about what the other person finds so troubling in your proposed action or the other alternatives he is discarding. For example:

"I'm not sure I understand exactly what you're seeing as a problem."

"Can you be more specific about why this is such a bad idea?"

Remember that in the eye-opening game of help, you don't score any points for converting the other person to your point of view. The way you do score is by the number of new ideas or insights you can get the other person to bring up. The best way to do this is by encouraging the other person to tell you more, to convince you further about his position.

Now, it can develop that you feel the other person is way off target. For instance, you may feel he isn't even discussing the issue at all, or you may find he persists in trying to force his conclusion on you again and again. In other words, it is not merely a matter of your disagreeing with the other person's position. It's much more serious. You really aren't getting anything you find very helpful. Whether or not it's your fault that you are getting nothing is beside the point. You feel you have to do something to change the character of the conversation. What you can say is something like this:

"You may be right, but I'm having trouble accepting it (or seeing how to use it). Could we try a different approach?"

The key is to avoid stating, at least directly, that you feel the other person is wrong or that his ideas are not valid; instead you take responsibility for the difficulties. It is you who cannot find

a way to use the idea, not that the idea (or the other person) is
bad or wrong.

Seek Out Specifics

Typically the other person's comments will start out on a
somewhat general plane—too general to provide many eye-openers. It is when you push for specifics that the new information
and novel possibilities start emerging. For instance, say you are
asking advice of the neighborhood car buff about which new car
you should buy. After he gives you his recommendation (probably along with a few of the benefits of that particular brand), ask
him for more specifics about the mileage, the kinds of repairs
required, how he decided to buy that brand of car himself (if he
did), and so on. (For more on techniques for getting specifics, see
chapter 2.)

Once you have unlocked the flow of specifics, you may find
yourself flooded with too much information or too many ideas to
assimilate—not a bad problem to have. It is then easy for you to
say something like this:

> "Slow down a minute, could we just focus on . . . ?"

In Quest of Qualms

Much of the detail the other person gives you may be a bit
one-sided, ideas or information that support his point of view.
You can get a lot of additional eye-openers if you just *ask the other
person for arguments on the other side.* This is quite different from
providing the opposing views yourself. Try a phrase like this:

> "I know there's no perfect solution, but what kind of
> problems do you think I might run into if I followed
> your advice (or that alternative)?"

Notice you don't ask *whether* there would be any problems, because that makes it all to easy for the other person to reply with
a simple no. Instead you imply that every position (including his)
probably has some negatives as well as positives.

Avoid Logic Chopping

It usually doesn't pay to point out the inconsistencies or other logical flaws in what the other person is saying—at least not in the early stages of the discussion. You might want to jot down a note about the flaw, however, so that you don't brood on it and miss the rest of the conversation. Don't forget that you have probably spent a good deal of time thinking through your problem, while the other person may be diving in cold. The other person may have some knowledge or expertise that you don't, but usually you know much more about your problem than the other person does. So your helper may need a bit of time to figure out what she really thinks, and even then her comments may come out sort of half-apt. Yet, as was noted before, it can be precisely the other person's newness to your problem that helps produce the useful eye-openers.

Later on in the discussion, then, you may want to bring up the logical holes you noticed. It is at this later stage that raising such logical issues may help produce further new ideas and insights. In any case, remember that the point is not to prove the other person wrong (logically or otherwise), the goal is to stimulate the production of eye-openers.

Thank Your Helper

Obviously you should thank your helper, not only out of common courtesy but also as a way of cultivating a future source of assistance. Thanking your helper may not produce more eye-openers during the current conversation, but it can certainly motivate the other person to make himself available for giving you help in the future (and who are you to say you won't need it?). How to make your thank-you effective and not just perfunctory may not be so obvious. Giving a thank-you is much like giving a credit or praise, and the difficulties are much the same: deciding what it is you want to give thanks for and making the thank-you believable. The techniques covered in chapter 4 are all highly relevant to giving thanks.

USEFULNESS DOESN'T EQUAL USAGE

> "If I've been so helpful, then why aren't you following my suggestions?"

This is a common (if unexpressed) sentiment that points up one frequent difficulty in thanking someone effectively for his eye-opening advice. In fact, you may be asking yourself the same question—"How can I sincerely thank him, since I don't really plan to adopt (or accept or use) his recommendation?"

This problem again stems from the common set of expectations about advice, namely that good advice consists of coming up with definitive solutions, answers, or conclusions. Hopefully, you now realize that the other kind of eye-opening help can be very useful, but the other person may still feel he hasn't really helped unless you fully accept (or agree with) his point of view. That other person probably also views your reaction to his advice as an all-or-nothing matter. So you may be delighted with the one or two eye-openers you have received (and may even plan to use), but the other person may be brooding over all the other ideas and opinions that you did not seem to pick up on.

As a result, you may need to spend a minute or two explaining the importance of eye-openers, how a conclusion can provide a fresh insight even when you don't completely agree with the conclusion. The important thing for you to do is to mention one or two specific, useful ideas or insights you got from the conversation—mention them even if they didn't come fully out of the other person's mouth, because they still count as something you didn't have before the conversation. Then you can deal with the parts of the advice you didn't agree with. You may want to comment along these lines:

> "You know, even though I didn't agree with some of your ideas, they were new to me, and they made me rethink the situation."

> "Even though I haven't accepted all your ideas, your comments really helped clarify the problem for me."

> "I don't fully buy some of your thoughts, but they did trigger some very useful, new ideas of my own."

Again you should probably provide a specific example or two after such a phrase to clarify what you mean.

You know, even getting absolutely nothing new is often useful too; it is confirming (if not conclusive) evidence that you have not overlooked some obvious, important point. So you can still thank your helper for assisting you to think through the situation carefully or for helping you feel more confident about the decision or action you plan to take.

Now, here is the sample dialogue mentioned earlier. The dialogue demonstrates the techniques for getting eye-openers in an actual situation, and it covers most of the approaches suggested in the preceding section.

Sample Dialogue—To Illustrate Use of the Techniques for
Getting Eye-Opening Advice

Joan is discussing a new job opportunity with her friend Mildred over a cup of coffee.

JOAN: So anyhow, that's the story. They want me to take over the typing pool; and it means more money and responsibility. But I just don't know whether I ought to take it. I know you can't make the decision for me, but you've had a lot more experience in organizations than I have. I'm hoping you'll be able to give me some new insights on this thing. I mean you might be able to point out some things that I haven't considered.

asks straight out for eye-openers and emphasizes the "something new."

MILDRED: Well, I don't know, but it sounds like a pretty neat opportunity, and there aren't always that many chances to move ahead like this.	(draws conclusion)
JOAN: It sounds like you think I really ought to accept the job, then. Right?	listens to conclusion and tries to paraphrase
MILDRED: Absolutely. I mean I'm assuming you know who your new boss would be, and that you think you could work well with him.	(notice ideas and insights popping out)
JOAN: So you feel if the boss looks okay, it would be a good move for me?	still listens and tries second paraphrase
MILDRED: Yeah, you could certainly handle the job, and you can't really afford to pass up an opportunity like this.	(insists on her opinion)
JOAN: Well, that's very interesting . . . very interesting	stifles own reaction and uses cop-out phrase
MILDRED: I just think you'd be downright silly not to take this job, but of course it's your decision.	(personal slur)

JOAN: I know that, but the thing is I'm not really clear about why you feel it would be so bad to stay where I am for a while longer.

responds to slur by asking for more detail

MILDRED: Okay, for one thing I don't think you ought to stay in your present job too much longer. You haven't really been a manager yet, and you've got to broaden your experience.

(ideas and insights emerge)

JOAN: Why not stay? I mean what would happen if I did?

probes for more specifics

MILDRED: Oh, it's awful easy to get typecast (if you'll pardon the pun), and I know your boss thinks highly of you, and that makes it even more likely that you'll get locked in. Once you've turned down a few offers, you'll find they stop coming your way. And also I hear the company is really hurting for good female managers, and they've had a lot of trouble with the typing-pool personnel, and—

(more insights and information tumble out)

JOAN: Whoa, hold on a second, can we just go back to this business of my present boss for a minute?

slows Mildred down and tries to focus in

MILDRED: Sure! Good secretaries aren't easy to find nowadays, and your boss is likely to do whatever he can to keep you.

JOAN: That may be, Mildred. I mean I know there's no ideal answer. But what sort of problems do you think I might run into if I did leave my boss and take the other job?

asks Mildred for arguments on the other side

MILDRED: Oh, I suppose you might have some trouble getting those young college grads in the typing pool to keep their nose to the grindstone, but I'm sure you could handle it.

JOAN: Maybe, but I wonder if you could give me a couple of examples of the kind of problems they're having now with the pool.

avoids comment on inconsistency between her supposed lack of managerial experience and Mildred's assertion that she could handle a difficult managerial situation

MILDRED: Well, I'm not sure, but I gather their system for allocating the work load is not very good. And you know, the managers always want their work done yesterday.

JOAN: Look, I have to run. You know, this has really been very helpful. You brought up some new issues that I really hadn't thought much about before. Like my boss maybe keeping other opportunities from coming to me. And I wasn't aware of the work load problem in the secretarial pool. I'm not sure I agree with all your conclusions, but your comments certainly helped me rethink the situation. Anyhow, I'm certainly going to do some more thinking on this thing based on some of your ideas. Thanks again for working on this with me.

thanks Mildred and explains the importance of eye-openers

provides a few examples of what was useful

explains that even things she didn't agree with were also helpful.

MILDRED: No problem. I'm glad to
help. Isn't that what
friends are for? I'll be
interested to know how
you come out on this
thing, and I'll probably
see you next week at
the Ludwigs'.

(seems to feel she was
helpful, even though Joan
didn't necessarily agree
with her conclusion)

THE COMMON THREADS

*Acknowledge the other person's conclusion; don't worry about whether or not
you agree with it, but instead use it to generate ideas, information, instruction,
or insight.* These are the common threads that tie together the
various techniques for getting eye-opening advice. The approaches are designed to produce new input for your thinking
about a problem, but they leave the ultimate responsibility for
deciding on a solution or action with you.

By looking for eye-openers instead of moral support or definitive answers you will find substantial payoffs:

- You make more progress with your problem—you will
understand your problem better, clarify your conflicting desires, develop a better plan of action.
- The other person feels more helpful—he is less frustrated when you don't agree with everything, less confused about what you really want, more often pleased
at having made a tangible contribution to your thinking.
- More people can be of help than you thought—because
the emphasis is on searching for different ideas, each
person's differences from you become a potential for
eye-openers instead of disagreement.

An intriguing eye-opener about the whole subject of getting
help is provided by the Japanese style of making important business decisions. (You see how eye-openers can come from differences?) Apparently, when a major business problem arises, it is

discussed and rediscussed at all levels of the Japanese organization. But the emphasis is on elaborating the problem, teasing out all the issues and alternatives, discovering all the pros and cons of each alternative. Reaching a consensus on any particular solution is actively discouraged until some organizational agreement is first reached on the full definition of the problem and the possibilities for action.

In somewhat analogous fashion, the eye-opening approach to getting help is perhaps best described as problem-oriented rather than solution-oriented. The emphasis is on learning more about the problem or situation and the potential alternatives than it is on reaching agreement about the ultimate solution, decision, or action. And perhaps because this approach may be a bit "foreign," you may have to put in a bit of extra work, on both ends —getting the other person to give you the eye-opening kind of advice and then making use of it in your own thinking. But then, nobody said you wouldn't have to help your helper help you!

Following is a "help full" chart that summarizes most of the major ideas and techniques discussed in this chapter.

SUMMARY CHART ON HELP

Help in the form of
advice or counsel

*Answers
Decisions
Conclusions*

Moral Support
potential conflict in
asking for honest opinion
and for approbation
at the same time

difficult to
get
because
other
person
isn't you

Eye-Openers
ideas, information,
instruction, insights

best split into

desire for emotion-al warmth or sym-pathy	desire for confir-mation of own position
ask for it	express hope for it but don't request it

1. Ask specifically for the four i's and explain difference from other two kinds of advice.

2. Don't fill in too much detail too soon, or you'll overload the other person.

3. Prove you hear the other person's conclusions through use of paraphrase.

4. Stifle any strong reaction of agreement or disagreement. Use a neutral cop-out phrase and/or push for more detail.

5. Seek out specifics.

6. Ask the other person for arguments that go against his position.

7. Avoid logic chopping, at least early on.

8. Thank your helper, and include explanation of how he has helped (with examples) even though you don't agree with or plan to use everything he said.

6 All About Everything You've Always Wanted to No

"Horse Sense" might be summarized as knowing when to say "neigh."

———ROSEMARIE WILLIAMSON

YES IS A PLEASANT COUNTRY; NO'S WINTRY*

- A cosmetics salesperson tries to sell you a special sampler kit at your door (or in a store).
- Your child asks for help with his homework.
- Your boss delegates some specific assignment to you.
- A friend asks you to baby-sit or to drive him someplace.

All these are examples of another person asking you for something: money, advice, help with a task, information. We might call them demands to which you may say yes or no. Saying no to such demands is the subject of this chapter. We will not be talking about the no involved in disagreement, that is, the negative response to the question "Do you agree?" (For thoughts on handling disagreements, refer back to chapter 3.)

*Adapted from the first lines of an e. e. cummings poem, "yes is a pleasant country. / if's wintry."

Typically another person asks you for something in order to help him fulfill a need or want. Your saying no poses a problem for the other person because his need or want remains unfulfilled. So you may often feel uncomfortable about saying no. When you say no, you risk experiencing the other person's anger, frustration, or at best his disappointment at being thwarted. Your no can even cause the other person to lower his general opinion of you or cause him to like you less. Also, you may feel that there is an implied quid pro quo, that saying yes will get you love, a reward, or praise in return. And don't forget that the other person didn't make his demand of just anybody, he made it of you!

Margaret Matlin and David Stang have written up a list of some twenty-two generalizations that emerge from their research and the research of others on what they call the Pollyanna Principle.* Here are a few of their pertinent generalizations:

- People seek out the pleasant and avoid the unpleasant.
- People take longer to recognize unpleasant or threatening stimuli.
- In general, people obey the monkey that urges them to "speak no evil"; they communicate good news more frequently than bad news.
- Pleasant words are used more often in the English language than unpleasant ones.
- When people make lists of items, they put pleasant items first.
- People tend to think about pleasant items more often than unpleasant items.

Well, you get the idea. And the fact is that usually no-news is bad news, that is, unpleasant for the other person. No wonder that your saying no can feel dangerous.

*Margaret Matlin and David Stang, "The Pollyanna Principle," *Psychology Today* (March 1978).

Your boss may not always be right,
but he is always your boss!

Orders and Requests

It is one thing to risk another person's displeasure and quite another to risk your job or life. If your boss threatens to fire you unless you do something, even the nicest, warmest no may not be a real option. If a holdup artist asks you for your wallet, you should probably not contemplate any form of no. If by saying no you break the law or a legal contract, it may not matter much how you say no. In all these situations, the demands are of a particular type that might be called orders. And in the presence of an order, the price of saying no gets very high.

Much of the time, however, demands are of another type that might be called requests. Now, the other person certainly has the right to make a request (almost any request). But, then, on the other hand, you have the right to say no. It is true that sometimes orders are disguised as requests. More often than not, however, what happens is that *you react to a request as if it were an order,* particularly if the request comes from someone with apparent authority. Thus, you may imagine more risk in saying no than a particular request really warrants.

A good example of how a request can be mistaken for an order is provided by the typical employment application form. Somewhere on such a form there is always a question about previous salary. Now, we all know that the main purpose of that question is to help an employer judge what compensation to offer, and thus avoid overpaying. Answering this question rarely works to our advantage, yet even experienced managers feel compelled to answer such a question (although they may add a few bucks to their answers).

The point is that if you perceive the questions on an employment form as requests, then you will realize you have a right to say no, not to answer some of them. (Incidentally, a few successful managers never provide any salary information on a form. Instead they provide the salary level desired, a good example of the "say what you will do" technique to be discussed later.)

So when you are contemplating a no, the first thing to do is to decide whether the demand is basically an order or a request. If it is a request, then some of the techniques that follow may help you say no. The techniques won't turn your no into pleasant country, but they can make your no much less wintry.

EVERYBODY'S GOT TO NO SOMETIME

Know What You're No-ing
"Mommy, I need you to help me with my math homework."

"Is it possible that you could stay a bit late tonight to finish up that Sappho contract?"

These are clearly requests, but requests that aren't clear. Does the child need help in figuring, or does he not understand the concepts, or does he just want the answers? Similarly, it is not clear why the boss needs you to stay late: Is the Sappho contract that important; what will happen if the contract isn't finished; how late are you supposed to stay?

As with so much other communication, the most important thing about requests is understanding them. And as usual there can be two causes for faulty understanding: You may not fully understand the request, but also the other person may not have thought through fully what he is asking for. The other person may not know exactly what he needs or what the alternatives for getting it might be. So even before you check your understanding, you may want to ask for a little more information (perhaps using the techniques suggested in chapter 1 for getting the other person to say some more). You also may want to probe for some specifics (using some of the techniques suggested in chapter 2).

ACKNOWLEDGE THE NEED OR PROBLEM
Behind any request is some sort of need or problem. Be sure you understand not only the other person's demand but also the need or problem behind the demand. At the very least, you should understand and acknowledge that the other person does

have a need or problem, even if you aren't completely clear what it is.

Sometimes the other person will preface his demand by explaining his bind or problem. Often, however, the need is left unstated, and you may have to go digging for it. If you don't understand the other person's problem, then his demand can sound very arbitrary. And more important, your no may sound equally arbitrary. On the other hand, just because you acknowledge the need or problem doesn't mean you are then obliged to fulfill his demand. You don't even have to agree that there is a problem. What you do have to do is accept the fact that the other person thinks he has a problem—because he does think he does.

TRY PARAPHRASING

The paraphrase techniques described on page 21 are a good way to make sure you know what you're no-ing, and they will also help make your no less frosty. In this case, your paraphrase should probably have two parts: one for the need or problem and one for the demand. For example,

> 1st: "Before I react, let me make sure I understand; your problem is . . ."
> 2nd: ". . . and what you'd like me to do is . . ."

Using the phrase "before I react" may be important to avoid leading the other person to assume that by restating his problem and demand you are about to say yes.

Now, as you check your understanding, you are likely to become more sympathetic to the other person's demand (although still not willing to fulfill it). You might in this case then want to preface your no with a phrase like this:

> "You know, I really don't blame you for asking (or wanting) . . ."

What you usually want to avoid in your no is any implication that the other person had no business making the request in the first place. So avoid something that sounds like this:

- "You know, you *shouldn't* ask me to do something like this."
- "You *have no right* to . . ."

If, on rare occasion, you feel the other person's demand breaks a previously agreed-upon rule, then you can say something like "Didn't we agree that we wouldn't ask each other to . . . ?" But use this approach sparingly.

Remember that the other person has a right to request almost anything—and you have a right to say no. Saying no is a different matter from liking or not liking that the other person made the demand, and saying no is different from agreeing or not agreeing that the other person's problem is really a problem. But in any case, before you say no, check your understanding—if only because a no is risky—in order to ascertain whether the demand is more of an order or a request.

Clarify Your No

It helps to know what you are no-ing, but it's also worthwhile to let the other person know more fully what your no means. For instance, a bare-bones no can all too easily be interpreted as a no forever. So you may want to preface your no with a phrase like one of these:

"*Right now* I can't . . ."

"*At this moment* I don't see my way clear to . . ."

Forever is a long, long time. Even if you don't think you would ever say yes, you don't really know what the future will bring. Making your no apply only to the here and now will make it a bit less harsh.

In similar fashion, an unqualified no might also be interpreted as applying to a wide range of related requests under all conditions. And this kind of general interpretation could make the other person more annoyed about your no than need be. So be specific in explaining that your no relates to this *particular request* and these *specific conditions.* For instance, it isn't that you are unwilling ever to stay late no matter the task. It is this particular request to finish up the Sappho contract this night to which you are saying no. (Notice that clarifying your no does not necessarily mean defending or justifying it; but more about that later.)

SAY WHAT YOU WILL DO

One important way of clarifying your no is to say what you will do along with what you won't do—what you are saying no to. You may not be willing to fulfill the other person's request fully or exactly, but perhaps you can do something helpful nevertheless. For instance, you decide to say no to baby-sitting for your friend, but you might still suggest someone else who could baby-sit. You might not be willing to finish up the Sappho contract tonight, but you would be willing to come in early the next morning. Such suggestions not only clarify what you are no-ing, but they also demonstrate that you really do understand that the other person has a problem or need, one which doesn't disappear because you say no to his request.

Sometimes the best you can offer is what might be called a "definite maybe." Even if you feel reasonably certain that your later answer will be a no, you can say something like this:

"I'd really like a little time to think it over."

In this way you avoid an outright no. And who knows, with the passage of time, the other person's problem may fade, or he may find another way of solving it. But use this approach judiciously, or else the other person will soon feel you are always just putting him off.

The Techniques in Action

Here is a somewhat extended specific example of saying no that demonstrates the use of most of the techniques discussed so far:

> Bill stops by Sharon's desk at work to ask her if she would play tennis with him Saturday morning. Sharon was looking forward to sleeping late on Saturday and then working in her garden before meeting a friend in the early afternoon. Bill is Sharon's boss.

Observations

BILL: Good morning, Sharon. I'm
sorry to interrupt.

SHARON: Oh, that's okay. What's
up?

BILL: Well, I'm in a bind. We
really need a fourth for
doubles this Saturday, and
I've heard you play a lot of
tennis. So I'd really
appreciate it if you would
come play with us.

SHARON: Umm . . . golly, I did   probes for more
have some plans. . . . Is   information
there something special
about this?

BILL: The thing is that one of our
major suppliers is in town
with his wife, and I
promised to take them to
the club for some tennis.
The guy is a real tennis nut.

SHARON: My, it does sound like   acknowledges the problem
it's important to get a
fourth.

BILL: Oh, come on, you'll enjoy
it, and I don't want to
disappoint the guy.

SHARON: I gather you'd want to   decides the demand is not
play for an hour or so, is   an order but a request,
that it?   albeit an important one;
                                checks out understanding
                                of what the request entails

BILL: Yeah, the club lets us
reserve the court for an
hour and a half on the
weekends if it's for doubles.

SHARON: So, essentially it would   further checks out the
end up taking most of   request
the morning, right?

BILL: I guess so, by the time we
have a drink afterward.

SHARON: Frankly, I really would   says no and clarifies
prefer it if you could   application to this specific
find someone else. I sort   instance
of don't want to knock
out the whole morning
this particular Saturday.

BILL: Boy, it's going to be hard to
find anyone else, I'm afraid.

SHARON: I'll tell you what, why   gives a definite maybe
don't you check around
and see if you can find
someone else and then
check with me later
today? I really don't
want to lose the whole
morning, but if you get   says what she will do as
completely stuck, I'd be   well as what she won't do
willing to play for an
hour and then cut out.

BILL: Okay, let me get on the
phone and see what I can
do. I'll get back to you this
afternoon.

"I Can't" Versus "I Don't Want To"

"I can't" leads to

  "Why not?" which leads to

    "Because . . ."

Thus, if you say no with some form of "I can't," you usually end up having to supply reasons for your no. And sometimes there are good reasons for supplying reasons:

1. You may have good and sufficient reasons.
2. Your reasons may be of the type easily understood and accepted by the other person.
3. The context may be one that seems to require reasons.

So far as the context is concerned, for instance, many business situations require that you give at least the appearance of functioning in the rational mode, that is, that you give plausible reasons for saying no. Much the same holds true for other kinds of organizations, such as hospitals or schools. Saying no without any explanation to your boss at the office may create a good deal of trouble for you, even if the boss is making a request, not issuing an order. It's not that the other person necessarily has to agree with your reasons, any more than you have to agree with his reasons for making the request. It is simply that both sets of reasons have to sound reasonable.

Another way to say no is by using some form of "I don't want to," though you may state it less blatantly. Notice that this approach implies that *you choose* not to; whereas the "I can't" approach suggests that *external events force you* not to. The "I don't want to" approach does not have to be backed up with reasons. You just say something like this:

"No, I'd rather not."

If you find yourself still pressed for reasons, then you can reply with one of these phrases:

"I can't give you a specific reason."

  "I don't know why exactly, it just doesn't feel right."

    "I'd really prefer not to give you any reasons right now."

In certain cases you may also be able to use this statement if the other person becomes really insistent to have reasons:

> "I do have some reasons that are quite personal, and I'd rather not discuss them."

In general, we tend to feel that reasons are required, although in many contexts they are not. For instance, plenty of highly regarded performing or creative artists say no quite often and get away without providing good reasons. A good, trusted friend or a close family member may accept a no without good reason (and still remain your friend). Not all business situations require reasons either. For example, in certain stages of negotiating a business deal or contract, it may be better not to supply reasons (or at most supply only vague ones).

Even in a situation that seems to require reasons, there are times when you are better off not supplying reasons. If you don't have good reasons or if your reasons are highly personal or if your reasons may be difficult for the other person to understand, then the "I don't want to" approach may be preferable. Such was the case with Sharon in the dialogue above. Notice that she essentially chose the "I don't want to" gambit rather than the "I can't" approach.

If you don't have reasons or don't want to expose them and you still elect the "I can't" approach, then the tendency is to manufacture reasons or else rely on one of the standard excuses from the reference list provided below.

Table of Standard Excuses

To save time for management and yourself, please give your excuses by number.

1. "That's the way we've always done it."
2. "We tried it before, and it didn't work."
3. "That's not my department."
4. "I can't do that until I get an okay from the chief."
5. "That's not my job. (I wasn't hired to do that.)"
6. "Wait till the boss comes back and ask him."
7. "I'm so busy, I just don't have time."
8. "The timing is really bad on this."
9. "I have a headache."
10. "My in-laws are arriving for an eight-week visit."

The trouble with manufactured reasons or standard excuses is that they often do not sound very reasonable, and that is likely to annoy the other person severely. Even if they sound reasonable, the tendency will be for the other person to try to argue you out of them; and defending your manufactured reasons can get very dicey.

No, No, a Thousand Times No

All right, when the other person makes a request of you, she does so because she has a need or problem, and she has picked you for a reason. In short, the other person is not typically prepared to take no for an answer (even when she suspects you might indeed say no). So the odds are the other person will repeat her request, maybe several times.

But turnabout is fair play. As often as the other person repeats her request (and has the right to do so), so you are entitled to repeat your no. Not that you won't feel increasingly uncomfortable at having to repeat the no (which may also be why the other person chooses to keep repeating her request—a standard negotiating tactic, by the way). So you may find yourself reluctant to keep repeating your same words. You will feel compelled to find additional reasons, explain your no more fully, and so on. The trick is to remember that there is no reason why you cannot continue to repeat your same words (graciously, not impatiently) over and over again until the other person accepts them. This little phrase can help:

"I just don't know how to explain it any differently."

Repetition is really the most effective antidote for a repeated request.

> *"Just the place for a Snark!" the Bellman cried,*
> *As he landed his crew with care;*
> *Supporting each man on the top of the tide*
> *By a finger entwined in his hair.*
>
> *"Just the place for a Snark! I have said it twice:*
> *That alone should encourage the crew.*
> *Just the place for a Snark! I have said it thrice:*
> *What I tell you three times is true."*
> —LEWIS CARROLL

Well, no matter what you say, you won't turn no-news into good news. And some of the reaction to whatever you say will depend on how important the other person thinks his request is, on who that other person is, and on how often in the past you have said no. Still, when you gotta "no," you gotta no, but you do have options—ways of saying your no that can make a difference, and the summary chart that follows puts in one place all about everything you've always wanted to "no."

SUMMARY CHART ON NAY-SAYING

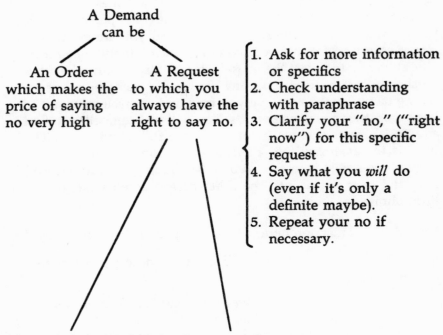

A Demand
can be

An Order
which makes the
price of saying
no very high

A Request
to which you
always have the
right to say no.

1. Ask for more information
   or specifics
2. Check understanding
   with paraphrase
3. Clarify your "no," ("right
   now") for this specific
   request
4. Say what you *will* do
   (even if it's only a
   definite maybe).
5. Repeat your no if
   necessary.

A Rational Context
"I can't"

compels giving
reasons and
explanation

An Emotional Context
"I don't want to"

may not require
giving reasons

7 Getting Personal—Speaking for Yourself

THE PERSONAL STYLE

Don't put yourself down.

Take responsibility for
your own wants and needs.

Don't be afraid to let
people know what you want.

Lose your mind, and
come to your senses.

Increase your
self-awareness.

Don't play "games."

Express your feelings.

Be more open.

All these are elements of a personal life-style, a style elabo-
rately described by a number of writers and researchers in the
field of what is now called humanistic psychology. These experts
believe that by following their tenets, you can feel much better
about yourself—more self-confident and less anxious or frustrated—and you'll be better able to realize your full potential.

The emphasis of the humanistic psychologists is on changing
your head around, that is, changing your self-image, working out
your personal needs, understanding yourself better. You may or
may not buy their basic message, and the purpose of this chapter
is not to sell you on their philosophy. The focus of this chapter
is to expose you to some interesting verbal options that have

emerged out of the more general thinking in the field of humanistic psychology. Many of these verbal approaches are rather novel and highly specific. They fit together loosely into what might be called a personal style of conversation, a style that is somewhat different from the way most of us talk most of the time.

There are two main components of this personal style, and each component is dealt with in a separate part of this chapter:

- Speaking for yourself, that is, putting a personal focus on what you say (discussed in the rest of this chapter).
- Expressing more of yourself, that is, the inclusion in what you say of wishes, feelings, or other material that often remains unexpressed (discussed in the next chapter).

In thinking about the personal style of conversation, don't be deceived by the word "personal." The verbal techniques in this chapter can be used in a great many situations beyond what you normally think of as intimate or highly personal encounters.

The personal style of conversation may indeed help you "get your head in a better place," but it can also provide a number of other more direct and concrete payoffs. If you are curious or concerned about these other payoffs, then read pages 165–168 now before you read the rest of the chapter, to learn the various techniques for getting personal.

Speak for yourself, John.
—HENRY WADSWORTH
LONGFELLOW

SPEAK FOR YOURSELF

Many psychologists have for some time asserted that what we take to be an objective reality "out there" is actually much more a projection of our own beliefs, needs, and desires. Even physicists and others in the hard sciences now freely admit that the observer always affects what is observed. And a good bit of research seems to show that our nervous system often can't tell the difference between an imagined experience and a "real" experience. In other words, a great deal of what we do, see, hear, feel, think is an individual experience that is never quite the same for anyone else.

> *When a pickpocket meets a saint, all he sees are his pockets.*
> —*attributed by* BABA RAM DASS *to one of his teachers*

That each person sees reality in his own way is precisely why speaking for oneself can be very important. If we all saw, felt, thought, and experienced the same thing at the same time, we would have precious little to talk about. Yet the separate, unique world views of each person can make our attempts to communicate very frustrating. Moreover, the conventions of the language we learn at school and use at home or on the job tend to ignore (or at least leave unacknowledged) the subjective nature of what we say. For example:

He: Watch out, you're driving much too close behind that car.
She: What do you mean? There's plenty of room.

Since we are all affected by the language we use, we begin to believe very strongly in our personal view of that reality out there that our language keeps referring to. We believe in it so strongly that we come to feel it is *the* reality. So if others don't see what we do, then they must be wrong or dumb (or maybe even crazy).

Unfortunately, the reality (if indeed there is any) is that only *you* can vouch for what you are saying, and someone else can agree or disagree or just plain not know what the devil you are talking about. In short, *we're always talking about ourselves, no matter what we're talking about.* Speaking for yourself as a verbal approach merely means explicitly recognizing this state of affairs.

> *People speak for themselves; facts never do!*

Now, please indicate your response to the question below:
Are you sexy or not?

- ☐ Yes, I am.
- ☐ No, I am not.

Please, before you read further, put a check mark in one of the boxes.

Chances are you were uncomfortable at being forced to answer this question—most people are. Some people are unsure; some of them bristle at feeling forced into one category or the other; and some tell the questioner to buzz off (or words to that effect). All of this, however, to get your curiosity (not your dander) up about the next section.

"To Be or Not To Be," That Is Not the Question

A study made some time ago by Wendell Johnson found that over "one-fourth of all the verbs in a total of several thousand written words were forms of only one verb." That verb was the verb "to be" plus its various forms, such as "I am," "you are," or "they are." "To be" is a convenient verb; you can put almost anything you want after it, and whatever you say sounds very authentic and factual. For example:

- "This stone *is* very smooth."
- "The Russians *are* the enemies of peace."
- "And that's the way it *was* today."
- "You *are* a very beautiful person."

If you want to speak personally, to speak for your<u>self</u>, then start by recognizing the effect of the verb "is" and the other forms of the verb "to be." Those verb forms make things sound impersonal and objective. The verb "is" forces things into an either-or framework. For example, either the stone *is* smooth, or it *isn't*. This is exactly why many people felt very uncomfortable about answering the "are you sexy?" question above; it must be interpreted as *are* you or *aren't* you sexy?

The either-or framework of an "is" statement is very conducive to argumentation. "Is you is or is you ain't my baby?" go the words of that old song. In more general terms this becomes "If you are not with me, then you must be against me." So if you want to start a disagreement, you couldn't pick a better verb than "is." (See pages 52–53 and 83–84.)

My daddy *is* a good worker (painter, teacher, or whatever).
No, he *is not.*

Yes, he is.
No, he isn't.

He is.
He isn't.

Is.
Isn't.

etc. . . .

Little kids argue this way a lot, but so do grown-ups—often
without realizing it. Perhaps a rose is a rose is a rose is a rose (at
least according to Gertrude Stein), but there are few "is" statements that are as undebatable as her tautology.

Using "is" makes you more combatible.

The other problem with "is" stems from its all-inclusive
quality. "He is a good (or bad) worker" implies that his work
is good (or bad) in *all ways all of the time.* Clearly such a judgment is likely to cause discomfort or disagreement, even if the
judgment is favorable, because the other person instinctively
knows he is not just one thing (even a good thing), and he
certainly realizes he is not that one thing all the time. You
see, the use of "is" means that you are stating an *attribute*
rather than stating a *personal reaction.* Besides, your one "is" is
never all there is. Nobody is just one thing. Also what you
say the other person is, is not necessarily what someone else
would say he is.

I am beautiful
You have quite good features.
She isn't bad-looking, if you like that type.

I daydream.
You are an escapist.
He ought to see a psychiatrist.

I am sparkling.
You are unusually talkative.
He is drunk.

—*Results of a conjugation contest*
in THE NEW STATESMAN AND
NATION

Several other related verb phrases that also put the other person in much the same bind as an "is" are these:

"should be"   "has to be"
"ought to be"   "needs to be"
"must be"

But more about these forms later. In the meantime, what if you want to make your comments a bit more personal, less either-or, less all-inclusive? What do you say?

Put in an Escape Hatch

Escape-hatch words, like the escape hatch on a submarine, leave the other person a way out and can thus soften the assertive quality of an "is." Chapter 3 already pointed out that the use of conditional words provides an escape hatch. For example:

"*Perhaps* you are . . ."
"*Maybe* it is . . ."
"*It could be* that they are . . ."
"He *seems* to be . . ."

These conditional or qualifying words make the "is" a bit less binding; they indicate that the situation might be otherwise than you believe.

Beginning of Wisdom *
I used to say Yes, No, Certainly—
With never a doubtful lapse;
But the longer I live, the oftener I say
Possibly, Maybe, Perhaps.
—MAY RICHSTONE

---

*Reprinted with permission of May Richstone and *The Wall Street Journal.*

Another kind of conditional word you can insert is a time qualifier. These qualifiers ameliorate the "forever" implication of an "is" statement. For example:

   "Sometimes you are . . ."
     "Right now it is . . ."
       "For the moment they are . . ."
         "When you did . . . you were . . ."

These words at least allow the possibility that the other person can be something else than what you say, at least part of the time. Otherwise an "is" (or an "isn't") can sound a lot like an "always" (or a "never").

Put Yourself Back in Your Statements

To combat the objective character of an "is" statement, all you need do is make clear that the statement is yours. Try one of these phrases:

   "In my opinion you are . . ."
     "For my taste it is . . ."
       "It seems to me that she was . . ."
         "From my point of view . . ."
           "To my way of thinking, it isn't . . ."
           "I guess (or estimate) that . . ."
          "I'm wondering whether . . ."
            "Looks to me as if . . ."

These phrases help make what you say sound like less of a universal truth, beyond all possibility of contradiction. They leave room for the other person to have her own opinion or reaction. Of course, whatever you say is only your opinion anyway. But explicitly acknowledging this every once in a while helps remind both you and the other person about the subjective nature of what you are saying.

An "I" for an I

A good way to speak for yourself is to make "I" statements, that is, substitute an "I" for a "you," "he," "it," "one," or "they."

For instance, in the confines of your boudoir your spouse or lover would find it a bit peculiar were you to say, "One loves you" or "You are loved." You would naturally tend to say, "I love you." Yet even in this highly intimate situation you still might say, "You are very attractive, you know" or "That nightgown is very sexy." If you were to truly speak for your*self*, you could say instead, "I find you very attractive, you know" and "I think that nightgown is sexy." After all, it is possible that someone else doesn't find your spouse or the nightgown attractive. And outside such a personal setting as the bedroom, you are even more likely to leave out the "I."

One reason you may not make many "I" statements may be that you were taught in school not to start every sentence with an "I." Other parts of the American culture also remind you frequently not to talk about yourself all the time (though there really is precious little else you can talk about). Then, too, it is sometimes just very convenient to act as if the "I" were not there. For instance, you may feel that the other person is more likely to be convinced by stating something as a seemingly objective truth than by stating it as merely your personal opinion. So for purposes of persuasion you may resort to an "it," "they," and so on. For example:

- "It is important to like your work."
- "They say that falling in love is wonderful."
- "Everybody knows that exercise is good for you."
- "Most people feel (or say) that . . ."
- "It's generally accepted that . . ."

And nowadays modern technology has provided an even better way to get yourself out of the picture: Just blame the computer. Ever try to get some clerk or manager to fix an error on your bill? Nobody is at fault, "it's just a computer problem."

Unknown Quantity *

There are two groups who set the pace
For things most people do.
I'd love to meet them face to face
Before my life is through.

They're specialists in all life's games,
Experts on rules of play
I only know them by their names;
They're—"Everyone" and "They."

—ELEANORE PADNOS

Incidentally, an "I" statement can often be substituted for an "is" statement. In fact it is possible to put an "I" back into almost anything you say (although you can, of course, overdo it). See whether you can get the knack of this by restating each phrase below so that it becomes an "I" statement. Just to make it a bit more challenging, follow these two restrictions:

- Use a different verb along with the "I" for each restatement.
- Do not resort to the "in my opinion" gambit.

Phrase

1. "That's a nice dress."
2. "This meat is overdone."
3. "You are so overemotional."
4. "You shouldn't smoke so much."

Your Restatement

1. I really like that dress.
2. I _____
_____
3. I _____
_____
4. I _____
_____

*Reprinted with permission of Eleanore Padnos and *The Wall Street Journal*.

5. "It's impossible to concentrate with all that noise."

5. I _____
_____

6. "How could you invite him?"

6. I _____
_____

7. "Most people wouldn't agree with you."

7. I _____
_____

8. "You really foul things up when you forget the keys."

8. I _____
_____

9. "My boss just doesn't spend enough time with me."

9. I _____
_____

10. "Let's drop the argument."

10. I _____
_____

If you didn't fill out most of the blanks, do go back and try it. The only way to add to your verbal repertoire is to try things out. And certainly writing in this book is one of the safer ways to experiment.

All right, below you will find at least one way of making an "I" statement out of each of the ten phrases listed above.

Phrase	*A Possible "I" Restatement*
1. "That's a nice dress."	1. "I really like that dress."
2. "This meat is overdone."	2. "I don't enjoy my meat cooked this well done."
3. "You are so overemotional."	3. "I think you get overemotional."

4. "You shouldn't smoke so much."

4. "I would prefer it if you did not smoke so much."

5. "It's impossible to concentrate with all that noise."

5. "I find it impossible to concentrate with all that noise."

6. "How could you invite him?"

6. "I wish you hadn't invited him."

7. "Most people wouldn't agree with you."

7. "I don't agree with you."

8. "You really foul things up when you forget the keys."

8. "I get really annoyed when you forget the keys."

9. "My boss just doesn't spend enough time with me."

9. "I believe I could do a better job if my boss spent more time with me."

10. "Let's drop the argument."

10. "I feel like dropping the argument, what about you?"

Most people who try making these restatements find that it requires some thought. The restatements are not all obvious, which only bears out how much we have adopted the habit of avoiding the "I" in our talk.

> *Think in terms of a line or fence*
> *between you and the other person.*
> *With "I" messages you are staying*
> *on your side of the fence, because your*
> *feelings are within your territory.*
> *With "you" messages you trespass*
> *into the other person's territory and*
> *hence invite defensiveness.*
> —GERALD WALKER SMITH

You may have noticed that your restatements as well as the sample ones here use such verb phrases as "I think," "I feel," "I wish"; and that leads directly to the second part of getting personal covered in the next chapter.

A summary of the verbal techniques presented in this chapter appears on pages 172–173. In the meantime, I hope you understand why "to be or not to be" is perhaps not the best way to word the question.

8 Getting Personal—Expressing More of Yourself

> Human speech conceals far more than it confides; it blurs much more than it defines; it distances more than it connects.
>
> —GEORGE STEINER

WHAT COMES AFTER THE "I"

At any one instant, you are experiencing many, many things: what you sense (see, hear, taste, touch, smell), what you want (desire or wish), what you feel (emotions), what you think or interpret, what you assume, what you expect. So there is no shortage of material for speaking personally. Not that you should always talk about all the elements, even to yourself. In fact, there is no way you can even be aware of all the elements at any one time. But the more elements of what you are experiencing that you work into your conversation, the clearer, fuller idea of yourself you give to the other person and the more personal you get. Here is a concrete situation:

> Susan's boss wants to have a large meeting to discuss better ways of handling customer complaints. The boss is asking Susan to set up the meeting and then chair it. Some of what Susan experiences during the discussion is listed below:

> She sees—her boss furrow his brow.
> She hears—him explain about the customer complaint
>   problem.
> She smells—the smoke from his cigarette (which
>   makes her slightly nauseated).
> She feels—a bit scared about running the meeting, and
>   also pleased at having been asked to do so.
> She wants—her boss to spend some time with her dis-
>   cussing the meeting agenda.
> She assumes—her boss has already told the others
>   about the need for the meeting.
> She expects—the boss to reduce her other work load
>   temporarily to give her time to deal with
>   the meeting arrangements.
> She acts—by taking notes as her boss talks.

Normally what Susan says would include only one or two of these elements. For example:

> "I know you feel this customer complaint problem is really serious, and I was thinking that with all those people I should sign up for the large conference room."

Here Susan is basically commenting on what she is hearing and thinking. If Susan wanted to express her_self_ more fully, she could include a few more elements by saying something like this:

> "I take it from your serious expression that you feel this customer complaint problem is really serious, and I assume you've communicated this to the others who'll be at the meeting. I must say I'm pleased that you've asked me to handle the meeting, although at the same time I'm a bit concerned about handling all those people. It would help me if I could check the agenda with you in a day or so, and in the meantime I thought I would sign up for the large conference room."

Do you see how this more personal approach lets Susan's boss know much more about what is on Susan's mind? If necessary, the boss can correct Susan's impression of the seriousness of the problem or her assumption about the other people being already informed. He can plan to spend time discussing the agenda now that he knows she would like that. He can help her with tips about running the meeting if he wishes to reduce her anxiety.

Probably 80 percent of what people say expresses just their thoughts. Most training in school stresses the importance of thinking ability—thinking clearly and logically (although some would describe it more as the ability to outwit the teacher). So the following sections will focus more on the other (nonthought) elements and provide suggestions for working them into your more personal conversations.*

Talking "Sense"

Our normal conversation usually includes some exchange of sensory information. We do talk about what we have seen or heard, what we have tasted, and to a much lesser degree what we have smelled or touched. For example:

- "Hank told me the other day that . . ."
- "Did you see on TV last night that . . . ?"
- "Have you heard about the new plan they're working on?"

But typically our sensory comments do not deal much with our *immediate* (right now) experience of the other person. For example:

- "I see you wrinkling your nose."
- "Right now you seem to be staring off into space."
- "You keep crossing and uncrossing your legs."

Perhaps we don't comment on such things because they are non-verbal, and somehow we feel that what we say should relate only to what the other person is saying. In truth, we all react very strongly to nonverbal behavior. Like it or not, someone frowning as we talk will affect what we say and how we say it.

---

*For an excellent discussion on including non-thought elements in your speech see chapters on the use of "the awareness wheel" in *Alive and Aware: Improving Communication in Relationships* by Sherod Miller, Elam Nunnally, and Daniel B. Wackman in (Minneapolis; Interpersonal Communications Programs, Inc., 1975).

Still, even though it is affecting us, why should we comment on what we see and hear the other person doing right now? Here is an example of how talking "sense" could significantly alter a conversation. First the more normal version:

SHEILA: Don't you like the stew I made?
HENRY: What do you mean? I think it's excellent.
SHEILA: Well, I don't know. You don't seem to be enjoying it.
HENRY: Of course I'm enjoying it. It's fine.
SHEILA: Are you sure? [that is, I don't believe you.]
HENRY: Yes, I like it. [that is, Damn it, stop bugging me!]

And from here the conversation could get very unhappy. Henry could get increasingly angry (but not talk explicitly about it), while Sheila could get increasingly upset that Henry doesn't really like the stew and, worse, is not telling her the truth. All the trauma might have been avoided if Sheila had said something like this:

SHEILA: I see you wrinkling your nose. Does that mean you don't like the stew?
HENRY: Not at all. I was just trying to figure out what you put in the sauce. I really like the taste, but it's quite different from what you usually do.

This technique might be called visual paraphrase, since it is a variety of the paraphrase technique discussed back in chapter 1. In that chapter, paraphrase was described as a way to play back what you *heard* in order to check out whether that was what the other person really meant (aural paraphrase). In the case above, Sheila is reporting back what she *sees* rather than what she hears, but the purpose is the same as for an aural paraphrase: to make sure she correctly understands what the other person meant.

This kind of visual paraphrase can be very important, because the other person may often be *unaware* of what he is doing nonverbally (much as what the other person says is not always what he means). Incidentally, you may also find it useful to *play back the nonverbal aspects of what you hear* as well as what you see. For example:

- "You are talking very loudly (or softly); does that mean . . . ?"
- "You are talking very rapidly (or slowly or deliberately)."
- "You seem to be weighing each word."
- "The pitch of your voice is very high right now."

When you paraphrase something nonverbal that the other person is doing, be careful to describe as neutrally as possible what you are sensing before you go on to interpret what it might mean. For instance, if you should say, "I hear a sneer in your voice," you are making an interpretation. You risk that the conversation will proceed like this:

> "I'm not sneering."
> "Well, you could've fooled me."

Even if the other person is sneering, he may not like it pointed out. And if the other person is, say, your boss, or just someone highly sensitive, perhaps you'd best leave all the interpretation to that other person. But notice that you can still feed back some of what you are seeing or hearing. Just make what you say more general and less interpretative, for example, "I notice that your expression just changed. Is there something I should know?"

The point is that nonverbal behavior means a lot, but the meaning is often very tricky to interpret. A number of popular books on body language imply that key gestures typically mean the same thing most of the time; for example, a woman who crosses her legs at a party is probably not very sexually approachable. But the most careful research studies have failed to uncover any single reliable meaning for a gesture even as simple as a smile. In fact, R. L. Birdwhistell found that the same kind of smile could have more than a dozen meanings (including displeasure) *depending on the context* in which the smile occurred. So it pays to check out what you see as well as what you hear.

By the way, the distinction between reporting and interpreting is equally important where the other senses of taste or smell are involved. For instance if you say, "This candy tastes awful (is no good)" or "It smells like you've burned the roast again," you are interpreting, not reporting. A more judicious way of expressing what you sense would be to say something like, "This candy tastes very salty to me" or "I smell something strange coming from the kitchen."

Once More with Feeling

Including some of your emotions in what you say is also an important way to make your conversation more personal. But just saying "I feel . . ." does not necessarily mean that you are expressing an emotional feeling. Take a look at the examples below, and see which phrases you think are true expressions of a feeling and which are not:

Does the Phrase Express an Emotional Feeling?

Yes	No	*Phrase*
☐	☐	1. "I feel terrific."
☐	☐	2. "I feel that you should spend more time with the kids."
☐	☐	3. "I feel uncomfortable about making a decision now."
☐	☐	4. "I feel mad when you don't finish things on time."
☐	☐	5. "I'm feeling really proud now about the way you handled that."
☐	☐	6. "I feel that this is very important."
☐	☐	7. "I feel we should all pull together on this campaign."
☐	☐	8. "I feel I'll be very content in the new job."

Of course, any of these statements could evidence an emotion if the phrase were spoken with a highly emotional tone. But so far as the words themselves are concerned, here is how many people have characterized each phrase.

Phrase	*Categorization*
1. "I feel terrific."	definitely an emotional feeling

2. "I feel that you should spend more time with the kids."

not really a feeling, more of a thought or a demand

3. "I feel uncomfortable about making a decision now."

feeling expressed is one of discomfort

4. "I feel mad when you don't finish things on time."

may have been an emotional feeling in the past when something wasn't finished on time; probably is not something being felt right now

5. "I'm feeling really proud now about the way you handled that."

seems to be an emotional feeling being experienced right now

6. "I feel that this is very important."

not really a feeling; more of a judgment or evaluation

7. "I feel we should all pull together on this campaign."

not really a feeling; more of a suggestion or exhortation

8. "I feel I'll be very content in the new job."

may be an emotion to be felt in the future, but at this point is more of a prediction

You can experience a vast range of emotional feelings: anger, fear, unhappiness, joy, confusion, depression, boredom, disappointment. As the above eight phrases demonstrate, the words "I feel" are no guarantee that what follows will express a true emotional feeling. An "I feel" phrase can express a thought or a judgment or a prediction or a number of other things that are not truly emotions. There is nothing wrong with such "I feel" statements, unless you think you are expressing a feeling when you aren't, for example, "My feeling is you're dead wrong!"

You will also notice that an "I feel" statement may not always express a current or immediate emotional feeling, something you are experiencing right here and now in this particular, present instance. When you talk about a past feeling or an anticipated future feeling, you are really expressing thoughts or reflections, not that it isn't sometimes appropriate to express such thoughts or reflections. Just recognize that the expression of a present emotional feeling has a much different effect from musing on some past or possible future feeling. Of course, reflecting on past or future feelings can make you happy or sad right now, and you might choose to express that present feeling as well.

Now that you know a little better what a present emotional feeling is and what it isn't, here are a few suggestions for effective ways to incorporate such feelings into what you say.

FEELING IS FIRST

Emotions are powerful and easily dominate thoughts or other elements of what you are experiencing. If you are really steamed up, if your feelings are really strong, then those feelings may be what you are most interested in and want to talk about anyway. Those strong emotions will make it difficult for you to pay real attention to what the other person is saying, and those same feelings will certainly color what *you* are saying.

Feelings do tend to come first, and yet they are rarely expressed explicitly first (or sometimes even last). You can try to bottle up the feelings, but often they ooze their way slowly, insidiously, into what you are saying. Because your feelings are not on the table, it can be difficult for either you or the other person to deal with them.

Thus, often you will find it useful to *express some of your feelings first*—get them out in the open. By laying those feelings (especially negative feelings) on the table, you will find you can move on more easily to the other ideas, problems, or opinions about which you are conversing. At a minimum you may feel better for having gotten the negative feelings off your chest. Also the other person will have a clearer idea of "where you are coming from" instead of sensing all the emotional undertones of what you are saying yet not knowing quite how to deal with them. In short, stating some of your feelings first can take a lot of guesswork out of the conversation.

ELABORATE A LITTLE ON YOUR FEELING

The trouble with expressing a feeling in just one emotional word or so is that you may not communicate very much. For instance, there are a few particularly overused general words that are so vague in their meaning that their use obscures or muddies what you are really experiencing. For example:

- "I'm frustrated."
- "I feel so embarrassed."
- "I'm really mad (or upset)."
- "I'm very happy."

You can convey your feeling more meaningfully by describing it a bit. How strong is the feeling? Where in your body do you experience the feeling—in your gut? in your neck? in your head? Using a metaphor or simile is also a good way to elaborate on your feeling, for example, "I'm as happy as the winner of a race"; "I feel so frustrated, it's as if I am being pulled in five different directions at once." And notice that your metaphor need not possess great poetic merit to provide effective elaboration of your feeling.*

FEELINGS DON'T HAVE TO BE JUSTIFIED

In our courts of law, the plaintiff must *prove* the guilt of the defendant; the scientific method is supposedly based on *objective* observation and *factual* evidence; most formal schooling emphasizes the importance of *thinking logically* and *being consistent.*

Little wonder, then, that you often feel compelled to justify

*Most of the thoughts on elaborating a little come from Sharon and Gordon H. Bower's book, *Asserting Yourself: A Practical Guide for Positive Change* (Reading, Mass.: Addison Wesley, 1976), p. 93.

your feelings in some sort of rational way. But the primary justification for most feelings is simply that you experience them. Often feelings know no reason, no logical or simple cause. You will have a heck of a time explaining your reaction to a sunset. Oh, you can point to the sinking sun that triggered your feeling, but that's a far cry from truly explaining your sudden feeling of calm, of being in harmony with the cosmos. And you certainly can't prove that a feeling is "right" (or even appropriate). So you will find it difficult to argue about a feeling or to change a feeling (your own or that of the other person). Often the best you can do is merely to acknowledge that the feeling exists.

> *The heart has its reasons which*
> *reason knows not of.*
>
> —BLAISE PASCAL

FEEL FOR YOURSELF

Getting personal means speaking for your*self*, putting your*self* back in your statements—and that includes those statements that reflect feelings. What does it mean to put your*self* back in statements that express emotional feelings? Basically it means that you express the feelings as your own, that you acknowledge that you are the one who creates your feelings.

Now, wait a minute. Obviously your feelings are yours, since clearly you are the one doing the feeling (which doesn't mean you have to like them). But it may not be immediately evident that you create your own feelings. In fact, don't you often attribute your feeling to what the other person says or does, for example, *"You* (the other person) make me mad when you forget the keys"?

Well, consider this slightly different perspective on how feelings are created. Events in the outside world are just events. They are essentially neutral. And what someone else says or does is also just one of those neutral events. You are the one that provides the reaction to, the judgment of, the feeling about the event. Moreover, as just noted, feelings are difficult to justify or explain.

About all you can say as to the origin or cause of a feeling is that it comes from you.

Whether or not you can control your feelings is beside the point. It is still you who makes yourself angry; more precisely, you notice yourself feeling angry when you discover that the other person forgot the keys. Someone else might not make himself angry. He might find it amusing or of no importance (if, say, he had brought along his own set of keys).

The perspective that you create your own feelings would lead you to say something more like this:

"I get mad [angry] when you lose your keys."

If you own your own feelings, then you leave the other person free to have her own feelings and actions, although certainly you will each have reactions to each other's feelings. But if you make the other person responsible for your feelings, you have given that person a responsibility she cannot handle very effectively. She can't control your feelings. Only you (if anybody) can.

SOMETIMES TWO FEELINGS ARE BETTER THAN ONE

Towering rage or ecstatic joy may temporarily blot out all other emotions. But most of the time, you are probably experiencing at least two different kinds of feelings and possibly more. The mere presence of these multiple feelings plus their possible contradictory nature can inhibit you from expressing any one of them. Talking about just one emotion can feel strange or wrong, inaccurate or incomplete. So instead you may decide not to talk about your feelings at all.

The other obvious approach is to go ahead and express several feelings. Doing this may seem difficult or awkward, but it need not be. You can use the format that was suggested for Susan back on page 146: "I'm pleased that you've asked me to handle the meeting, although *at the same time* I'm a bit concerned about handling all those people." Or you might want to use one of these phrases:

"Part of me feels . . . while another part of me feels . . ."

"On the one hand I feel . . . and on the other hand I
feel . . ."
By way of summary, a slight modification of that old chewing-
gum commercial seems unusually apt: Double your pleasure,
double your fun, try it with two feelings instead of just one.

The Feelings of Others

Feelings are very personal. If it is hard to become aware of (and
express) your own feelings, it is even harder to know the feelings
of others. Certain psychics do feel they have the ability to read
the minds of other people; and psychic is exactly what you are
claiming to be when you presume to *know* the other person's
feelings. Why not allow the other person to speak (and feel) for
himself?

Any comments about another person's feelings are guesswork
—your guesswork. And there's nothing wrong with guessing as
long as you let the other person know that you aren't presuming
to read his mind. Make it clear that you are *guessing* and that it
is *you* who is doing the guessing. You can do this by using any
of the techniques discussed previously for putting your<u>self</u> back
into what you say. For example:

"It seems to me you are feeling . . . Is that it?

"I notice . . . Are you feeling . . . ?"

Even if you are very sympathetic with what you believe the
other person is feeling, he may resent your intrusion into that
private realm, the realm of feelings; and of course, you might also
be wrong about what he is feeling. It is all too easy to fall into
the trap of "mind reading." For example:

- "I know just how you feel."
- "Boy, you're really uptight."
- "You're just feeling sorry for yourself, that's all."
- "You know, underneath it all you really do like your
  job."

In short, try the approach of *mind asking* instead of mind reading,
especially when you talk about the feelings of others.

> *Jill: I am frightened.*
> *Jack: Don't be frightened.*
> *Jill: I am frightened to be frightened*
> *when you tell me I ought not to*
> *feel frightened.*
>
> —R. D. LAING

DON'T TELL THE OTHER PERSON HOW TO FEEL

- "Don't worry! (Everything will be all right.)"
- "Oh, come on. (Don't feel that way.)"
- "There's no reason to be angry."
- "Relax, take it easy."
- "Getting upset only makes things harder, you know."

How many of us have used a phrase like one of these and felt we were saying something genuinely compassionate and personal. But R. D. Laing, the noted psychiatrist, points out the horrendous double bind created by telling the other person how to feel. On the one hand, we are telling the other person he is doing something wrong, doing something he shouldn't (or needn't) be doing, for example, worrying. On the other hand, the odds are it will be difficult for the other person to change his feeling. Feelings just aren't that controllable.

So now the other person is still worrying, and on top of that he is worried about worrying. In other words, if the other person agrees with us that he shouldn't be worrying, then he is left feeling guilty about worrying. And if he doesn't agree with us, then he may get angry at our telling him how he should feel. As Hardy used to say to Laurel, "Well, that's another fine mess you've gotten me into."

One way out of the mess is again to put the "I" back in what we say. For example:

"I wish you wouldn't worry."

"I get upset when I see you worry."

WHAT'S AN ENCOURAGING WORD?

Okay, so the other person opens up the conversation by saying, "I sure am feeling worried today." You care about the other person and are truly concerned about her being worried. You would like to help somehow if you can, or at least lend a sympathetic ear. You realize that saying "Don't worry" may create some problems. Which of the following responses would you be most likely to make? What do you think the effect of each of these responses would be?

1. "Why are you so worried?"
2. "Is something the matter?"
3. "How come?"
4. "What are you worried about?"
5. "You're feeling worried, eh?"
6. "I'm sorry you're feeling worried."
7. "You know, I've been feeling a bit down myself."

The fact is that any of these responses could be meant as a perfectly genuine, friendly, empathetic response. Yet using one of the phrases instead of another can produce a strikingly different response from the other person.

The first three phrases are certainly used quite often. But notice that they are all in the form of a question—a question that pushes for some kind of explanation or cause. In essence, the first three responses are all forms of a "why" question. And a "why" question has one guaranteed effect: It will tend to move the other person away from the territory of emotional feelings toward the rational domain of logical analysis, the territory of cause and effect. To answer a "why" question the other person must construct an explanation or develop reasons for her feeling. She must, in some fashion, diagnose what is going on. So don't ask a "why" question unless you want to push the other person away from feelings. (For more on the rational character of a "why?" refer back to page 32.)

Now, phrase #4 is also a common response in the form of a question, but it is a "what" question rather than a "why" question. As chapter 2, on getting specific, pointed out, a "what?"

probes into the structure of a situation rather than pushing for a cause-and-effect explanation. But even the "what" question still pushes for some diagnosis, some form of analysis. And much of the time the other person simply doesn't know exactly what is worrying her.

Phrase #5—"You're feeling worried, eh?"—represents a rather different kind of response from the first four. Basically, phrase #5 is a form of paraphrase, an attempt to feed back and check out what you are hearing and sensing. As discussed in the first chapter, paraphrase is a neutral kind of comment that proves you are paying attention, but a comment that leaves the other person relatively free to proceed in any direction she wishes. Often the reaction to a paraphrase is that the other person will say some more, that is, she will expand on her feeling.

Phrases #6 and #7 will also encourage the other person to expand on what she is feeling (rather than on why she is feeling it). These two phrases are not quite as neutral as the paraphrase of #5; they both include some statement of a *feeling of your own*. In phrase #6 you say, "I'm sorry," and in phrase #7 you say, "I've been feeling a bit down." For some reason, expressing a feeling of your own seems to provide the strongest encouragement for the other person to expand and explore her own feelings. Perhaps the reason is that expressing a feeling of your own signals to the other person that it is okay for her to continue talking about her feelings; after all, you are doing it, why shouldn't she?

Phrase #7 needs one bit of additional comment, because at first blush it seems like a strange way to encourage the other person to express feelings, that is, you are talking about a feeling of your own that is not directly related to her feeling. Indeed, phrase #7 will not encourage the other person to express her feelings if you use the phrase as a lead-in for dwelling on your own tale of woe. But if your intent is to draw out the other person, then this kind of phrase is the most powerful one you can use. You see, by talking about a personal feeling, the other person has exposed a bit of herself, and that can feel risky. When you respond with a feeling of your own, then you are also taking a similar kind of risk. So perhaps phrase #7 works because it helps establish an atmosphere of mutual trust in that you are both a bit exposed. Of course, the other person may still back off from further comment on her feelings; she may latch on to your problems instead. But if this occurs, chances are she really didn't want to discuss much further her own feelings anyway.

> *The universe is a projection of your desires.*
>
> —BABA RAM DASS

Wishes and Wants

As kids, we probably wished and wanted all over the place. As we grew up, though, we probably were taught to wish less (or at least to express our wishes less). But what happened to most of us is that we reduced neither our wishes nor our expression of them. Instead, we simply learned how to disguise our wishes so that they didn't sound quite as much like wishes. So our wishes and wants are rather tricky little devils. They keep popping up right and left, masquerading as something else. When we disguise our wishes, we risk irritating the other person, or at least confusing him (and sometimes ourselves in the process).

TURNING OBJECTIONS INTO WISHES

Wishes love to make themselves look like objections. The disguise is so effective that it takes a bit of digging to realize there is any relationship at all. Here is how to see the connection.

First, remember that objections are not objective truths; they are only opinions, subjective expressions of personal dislikes or disagreements. For example:

Objection	*Restated as a Personal Dislike*
1. "We just can't buy that new machine because it's too expensive."	"I don't like spending that much money for the new machine."

　　2. "Paris is too far　　　　"I would prefer not to
　　　　away for our　　　　　　go so far away as Paris
　　　　vacation."　　　　　　　for our vacation."

The next step is to realize that stating what you dislike is just the negative way of stating what you like,. what you want or wish for. Thus, the two objections above could also be restated in the form of positive wants or wishes. For example:

　　1. "I wish we had enough money to buy that new machine."
　　2. "I wish we could find a vacation spot that is closer than Paris."

As chapter 3, on criticism, pointed out, restating an objection as a personal dislike leaves room for the other person to state (or maintain) her own personal view. Going further and *restating the objection as a wish turns the issue into a problem to be worked on rather than a disagreement to be debated.* For example, your not wanting to spend that much money for a new machine could lead the other person to explain more about why it is important to spend that much money for the machine. Then you might find yourselves discussing how to raise the money; or perhaps you might explore how to make the new machine cost less, or develop alternative ways of accomplishing most of what the new machine was to do at a lower cost.

Of course, it's always possible that your stated objection is just an excuse and not what is really bothering you. But again, all this means is that there is some other wish you have lurking hidden in the background. Perhaps you feel this other wish is too irrational to express. Just remember that while objections are supposed to be rational, the nice thing about wishes is that they do not have to be.

WANTS AND NEEDS

Wishes and wants also like to dress up as needs. This disguise is tricky to penetrate because we all do have some true needs, things that we literally have to do rather than merely wish to do. Answer for yourself which of the following phrases probably expresses a true need and which phrases are more likely to be wishes dressed up as needs.

Wish	Need	Statement
☐	☐	1. "I really need a vacation."
☐	☐	2. "I have to spend more time with the kids."
☐	☐	3. "I need some fresh air. I'm going to faint."
☐	☐	4. "I have to change jobs."
☐	☐	5. "I have to take care of my invalid mother."

Perhaps you can conjure up an extreme situation for each of the above statements so that the statement would reflect a true need. Under most conditions, however, each of the statements, except #3, is most likely to be a wish masquerading as a need. One way to see this more clearly is to try rephrasing each statement by inserting an "I wish" or an "I want" to replace the "I need" or the "I have to"—"I really *want* a vacation" instead of "I really *need* a vacation." It is hard to find anything that is an absolute need, except for certain basic biological functions like breathing, eating, and so on.

In short, try *stating your "needs" as wishes or wants.* For instance, neither you nor the world will collapse if you don't spend more time with the kids or don't change jobs. Even taking care of an invalid mother may not be a true need, because there are always other options, such as hiring live-in help or putting the mother in a nursing home. If you do spend more time with the kids or change jobs or take care of an invalid mother, aren't you really *choosing* to do these things? Certainly your choices are constrained by the facts of the situation and by your resources. Clearly the choices may reflect compromises, that is, what you choose to do may only partially fulfill your want, or it may represent a choice from among a number of conflicting wishes.

So besides stating your "need" as a wish, you may also want to add this kind of phrase to your repertoire:

"I've chosen to . . ."

"I've decided to . . ."

In essence, choosing is a highly action-oriented form of wishing or wanting.

> *Your needs tend to control you, to "own" you, while you control and "own" your wants. Thus every need you can see freshly as a want begins to come under your control, becomes a choice rather than an imperative.*
> —NENA and GEORGE O'NEILL

WANTS AND "OUGHTS" OR "SHOULDS"

One last guise enjoyed by wants or wishes is the garb of "oughts" or "shoulds." Once again, the costume can create confusion, because any society abounds with supposed moral and legal imperatives. These "oughts" and "shoulds" represent codes of behavior imposed from outside us by some kind of authority, be it religious, governmental, cultural, or social. Civilization apparently needs such codes of behavior to survive.

A true imperative involves a command that is absolutely necessary and tightly binding, that is, it must be obeyed. Religious imperatives threaten you with eternal damnation, while legal imperatives threaten you with monetary fines or imprisonment for failure to obey. Yet how many of us strictly adhere to all the tenets of our religious faith? How many of us have never violated a law, never received a parking ticket? Certainly, the failure to obey some few imperatives can produce dire consequences, just as the failure to fulfill certain basic needs can cause serious problems. For the most part, however, neither you nor the world will fall apart because of your failure to obey a supposed moral or legal imperative.

So try *stating your "oughts" and "shoulds" as wishes or wants*. It is you who can decide whether or not something is an imperative, whether or not you wish to obey that imperative, and how to apply that imperative. Unfortunately the application of a specific imperative to a unique, personal situation is often murky at best. For example:

- "You shouldn't tease your brother that way."
- "I ought to be earning more money than I am."
- "We should write the Batesons a thank-you note."
- "We shouldn't keep the heat up so high."
- "One shouldn't cheat in filling out one's income tax forms."

How many of these are true imperatives for you, rules that you *must* obey? And how many of these are merely wishes or wants made to sound more objective and authoritative by the use of the words "ought" or "should"? You may categorize them differently than someone else. So make up your own mind (and speech), but realize that it is *you* who are making the choice.

> *An ethical man is a Christian*
> *holding four aces.*
> —MARK TWAIN

> *What is moral is what you feel good*
> *after.*
> —ERNEST HEMINGWAY

> *Moral indignation is jealousy with a*
> *halo.*
> —H. G. WELLS

"CANS" AND "CAN'TS"

These words are close relatives of the "shoulds" and "shouldn'ts."

- "I can't go out to the movie tonight."
- "I can't stay late tonight at work."
- "I cannot tolerate your running off without letting me know where you are."

A "can't" implies you are being forced into something by external events (over which you have little control). Sometimes this may be the case, but probably less often than most of us imagine. Often a "can't" is more accurately a "won't" or a "don't want to." For instance, you could go to the movies tonight but in fact you do not want to go strongly enough to overcome the difficulties involved—you don't want to go to the movies because you will be unprepared for work tomorrow or because you would prefer to watch your favorite TV program.

Again, you have to decide for yourself. Try *phrasing a "can't" as a "don't want to,"* for example, "I don't want to go out to the movie tonight." It may sound a bit curt, but it also may say more accurately and honestly what you are really feeling and thinking. (For more on the use of "can't" versus "don't want to," see page 128.)

> *Man blames fate for other accidents,*
> *but feels personally responsible when*
> *he makes a hole in one.*
> —HORIZONS *magazine*

PERSONAL EFFECTS: THE PAYOFFS FOR GETTING PERSONAL

You have been reading about techniques for getting personal —a style of conversation that is rather different from the way most of us talk most of the time. And, of course, that is the whole purpose of this book, to open up new ways you can talk. But what do these techniques for getting personal provide other than an offbeat option?

1. What you say becomes *more explicit.* Less is hidden or only hinted at. For instance, unexpressed feelings emerge indirectly, so that by including feelings in what you say you avoid forcing the other person to guess at them; the other person will be less likely to deal with those feelings incorrectly or covertly or not at all.

2. What you say becomes *clearer and more specific.* For example, talking about the nonverbal messages you are receiving is a way of pointing at something specific—a specific that is affecting what you say. Another example is that expressing a feeling as your own (and as created by you) is simply a more precise way of describing what is actually happening.

3. What you say becomes *more open,* that is, you allow more room for constructive disagreement. For instance, by avoiding the verb forms of "to be," you open the way for things to be other than you claim. Or by stating wishes as wishes instead of as needs or "oughts," you leave more room for alternatives; and notice that wishes don't "have to" be fulfilled.

Well, all this sounds terrific—for the other person. She gets things laid out on the table for her; she has more freedom to disagree; and so on. But why should you be doing all this for the other person? Why do this for the other person without some assurance that at least the other person will also do the same thing for you?

One immediate answer to these questions is simply that when you speak personally, you do increase the chances that the other person will adopt a similar approach. The odds go up if only because your getting personal implies that it is all right for the other person to do so. Your getting personal is an invitation or a permission to the other person to do the same thing if she knows how to or wants to.

Another line of response to the "what's in it for me" questions is provided by the quotes with which the first part of this chapter began. All those quotes assert that getting personal is a "good" thing, something you ought to do. You should take responsibility for your own wants and needs; it's good to express your feelings; you shouldn't play "games." Perhaps you agree with some of these ideas, perhaps you don't. (Ironically, one of the tenets of getting personal is that *you* decide what is good for you, and *you* choose what you have to or ought to do.) There are, however, other, more concrete payoffs for getting personal.

First, remember that when you talk, you talk as much to yourself as to anybody else. So talking personally does indeed help *you* (as well as the other person) know more explicitly and specifically where you are coming from, what you really feel or want, what you really can or can't do. And you leave more room for you to disagree with yourself, to deal with your own conflicting points of view. If you know better what you want, then you are more likely to get it. If you know better what you want, then the other person may be better able to help you get more of what you want. In short, getting personal *increases your chances of getting more of what you want.*

Second, getting personal is often a highly efficient form of conversation because of its directness. Problems are often solved more quickly when key personal issues are out on the table in quite specific terms and when you (and others) are open to exploring various options instead of being locked into only one possible answer or action.

Third, talking personally can *increase the level of cooperation* between you and the other person. Keeping things aboveboard, clear, and open creates an *atmosphere of trust.* The other person knows more about where you stand, and is therefore less likely to get bugged because she doesn't understand what you want, where you are coming from. This doesn't mean that the other person suddenly subordinates all her wants and needs, but she can work more easily on ways of meeting both her wants and yours.

Fourth (and even nicer), by getting personal you substantially raise the odds that *the other person will like you better.* This needs a bit of explanation. One standard fear about talking personally and revealing more of yourself is that the other person will know what's really there and will not like you if she sees what you are really like. That sounds logical enough, but there is a peculiar twist that causes the actual results to be quite different.

When you make general statements instead of speaking for your<u>self</u>, when you assert your subjective opinions as facts and truth, when you don't state your feelings but let them clandestinely creep in between the lines—when you do all this, you increase the odds that the other person will get upset, suspicious, worried, even mad. And when that other person experiences discomfort or anger or some other negative emotion, she is quite likely to blame you—blame you personally (particularly since she has probably not read this chapter and may not understand about taking responsibility for her own feelings).

When you talk personally, you remove much of the potential for discomfort in the other person. True, she may not like what she hears; she may not agree with your opinion or have no intention of fulfilling your wish. But your speaking personally makes it much easier for her still to like you as a person despite all the rest. When what you say is fuzzy, assertive, impersonal, then *it is much more difficult for the other person to separate her reaction to what you are saying from her overall reaction to you as an individual.*

There is one more potential benefit from getting personal: The conversation may simply be much *more pleasurable.*

When Getting Personal Pays Off

Expressing feelings, being open, and the other characteristics of the personal style are usually associated with an intimate relationship, a way of talking to your lover or family or close friends. But the personal style of conversation is quite applicable to many other situations, for example, talking personally to your boss, to your subordinates, to sales clerks, to service repairmen. This does not mean that you talk in identical ways with lovers and laundry men. You obviously get personal in a different way with your son than you do with a salesman.

The point is that the same techniques of getting personal can be applied to a variety of settings. And speaking personally is not necessarily a "soft" style. Getting personal can be a hard-nosed way of dealing efficiently with many on-the-job or other everyday problems of living. You can work the techniques into your criticisms and your credits. You can use it when you are coaching someone as well as chatting during your coffee break. For example, on the following pages is a transcription of a typical business discussion. To the right of the transcript is given an alternative way of saying some of the same things—an alternative that utilizes one or more of the techniques for getting personal that are summarized for you on pages 172–173.

Two Versions of a Business Dialogue

The left-hand column, below, is the actual transcript of a business conversation, the way it happened. The comments in parentheses indicate what the speaker is thinking, feeling, or showing, but not saying. The right-hand column suggests one way in which some of each speaker's statements might have been rephrased to get more personal. But the right-hand column does not represent a continuous alternative conversation. For instance, Sam's first response in the right-hand column is a response to how Bill actually started the conversation on the left-hand side; it is not a response to how Bill might have started the conversation (as rephrased in the right-hand column).

The raised numbers scattered throughout the right-hand rephrasings refer to the number of a specific technique for getting personal as listed in summary on page 172. The right-hand rephrasings incorporate most of the techniques listed in the summary, but not all of them.

Try reading the left-hand actual dialogue straight through first, so that you get a feeling for the conversation as a whole. Then go back and reread the actual dialogue, but stop and look at each alternate phrasing to see what difference it might have made.

Bill, a district sales manager for the Margrave Company, is talking in his office with Sam, a salesman hired some nine months ago. But the conversation could be any boss talking to a subordinate about a business problem. After some initial pleasantries, the talk gets serious.

BILL: Sam, I guess I'm not sure [I'm damn sure] how efficiently you're spending your time. We've just gotta get more efficient in this district, or we'll all be in big trouble.

Sam, I've got a problem.[4] Our district is way below quota for this quarter, and I'm worried.[7] The headquarters office is really getting on my back. What do you feel you can do to help the situation?

SAM: *(a bit miffed)* What are you getting at?

Well, I'm worried too, like a turkey gets before Thanksgiving.[8] But I resent[7] the implication that I'm wasting time.

BILL: Well, you just aren't getting around enough to the key accounts.

I've looked at your call reports[5] and it seems to me[3] that perhaps[1] you're calling on too many people outside our key accounts.

SAM: Okay, but you know there are only so many hours in the day, and I'm putting in a lot of extra hours as it is. *(notices boss wince)*

Look, I think[3] I'm working hard right now[2]. . . . I'm just noticing your expression, does that mean you don't agree?[12]

BILL: *(with great emphasis)* Yeah, but those key accounts are where the big bucks are!

SAM: Look, I admit I'm finding it rough going.

It sounds like you feel those key accounts are really the important ones, right?[6]

BILL: How come?

I know, I'm sweating a couple of tough accounts that I'm working on myself.[14, 15]

SAM: Well, you know, the competition is really heating up in our territory.

BILL: *(irately)* Sure, I know. That's why you just have to wrap up those key accounts.

I agree with you, and that is part of why I really wish[17] you could wrap up those key accounts.

SAM: *(objecting)* You make it sound like I'm not trying. I'm doing the best I can.

I wish I could do more.[16] Any suggestions?

BILL: *(with exasperation)* I don't know what to say. But we're gonna bring in more sales or else!

Hey, I get really upset[10] when[2] I hear you say there is nothing else you can do. I don't agree. There is always something else that can be done. Now, what I want is for our sales rate to pick up. I suggest you look over your list of accounts and rank them in some order of priority. Okay? And than get back to me.[20]

SAM: *(acidly)* Okay, boss, okay, don't get uptight. I'll keep rolling and do my best.

Okay, I realize you're feeling uptight.[13] I'll focus on those key accounts and see what I can do.

On the basis of this sample dialogue, do you see how the various techniques of getting personal can be worked into very un-intimate, even unfriendly kinds of situations? Can you see how the techniques can be used, even if the other person is not speaking personally? Did you notice that there were any number of places in the dialogue where getting personal would have made a constructive difference; where the more personal phrasing might have led to a very different response by the next speaker? For example, even toward the end of the actual conversation, if Sam or Bill had spoken more personally, they might have still parted not only more amicably but also with a greater likelihood of some appropriate action being taken to improve the sales situation.

SUMMARY LIST OF TECHNIQUES
FOR GETTING PERSONAL

Modify the effect of "is" statements (or other forms of the verb "to be").

1. Use conditional words such as "possibly," "perhaps," "maybe." ⎫
2. Use time qualifiers such as "sometimes," "right now," "when." ⎬ escape hatches

3. Put your*self* into the statement by using a phrase such as "in my opinion," "it seems to me." ⎫
4. Make "I" statements instead of "it," "you," "one," or "they" statements. ⎬ *owning* what you say

Talk "sense."

5. Comment on what you see. ⎫
6. Comment on the nonverbal aspects of what you hear. ⎬ forms of paraphrase

Include emotions in what you say.

7. Express feelings first—to get them out on the table.

8. Elaborate on your feeling a little through the use of metaphor or other forms of brief description.

9. Don't think you have to justify feelings.

10. Express feelings as your own, that is, not caused by the other person.

11. Sometimes it's easier and more useful to express two feelings instead of just one.

Deal with the feelings of others in these ways:

12. Don't mind read; mind ask instead, that is, make it clear that you are *guessing.*

13. Don't tell the other person how to feel, for example, "Don't worry!"

14. Don't ask a "why" question unless you want to push the other person away from feelings.

15. Express a feeling of your own to provide strong encouragement for the other person to explore his feelings.

Express wishes and wants.

16. Turn objections into wishes.

17. State most "needs" as wishes or wants.

you are making the choices or decisions

18. State most "oughts" and "shoulds" as wishes or wants.

19. State most "can'ts" as "don't want tos"

BONUS—A GENERALLY USEFUL SEQUENCE OF TECHNIQUES FOR GETTING PERSONAL (NOT SPECIFICALLY COVERED IN THE CHAPTER)

20. Express your feeling first.

Then follow with your agreement (or disagreement) with what the other person said.

Next make evident your want or wish.

Finally, suggest a possible or proposed action.

(For an example of this sequence in action, refer to the right-hand version of Bill's last speech on page 171.)

Well, then, should you conclude after all this that speaking personally is appropriate all of the time? Certainly not! Are there risks in getting personal? There certainly are! You can lose power over the other person. You may end up with less absolute control over the conversation. Sometimes laying your cards on the table will direct the other person's reaction too strongly; sometimes tipping your hand will allow the other person to take advantage of you, to hurt you more accurately and severely (if that is the other person's desire). Sometimes pinning things down and being too explicit creates premature disagreement or discourages a necessary consensus. Besides, some things just can't be pinned down early in a conversation; and sometimes opening things up too soon only results in confusion.

Such risks are present in speaking personally in intimate settings as well as in the more impersonal situations. But remember, there is another set of risks in not getting personal. So try out the various techniques that feel most comfortable. You'll find you can speak personally in many more situations than you initially thought possible. You'll find it pays to express more of yourself more often.

Getting personal makes you more
person-able.

9 What's Your Question?

A college student interrupted his philosophy teacher's lecture with this hoary but still perplexing question: "Professor, how do I know that I exist?"

Without a moment's hesitation the professor retorted, "And who may I say is asking?"

Why a Chapter on Questions?

Chapters 1 through 8 are each organized around a particular kind of purpose, something you want to get from or give in a conversation, such as understanding, criticism, or help. Among the techniques mentioned for achieving those purposes were various types of questions. Typically a question is used to help attain some other goal or purpose and is rarely an end in itself. So why a chapter purely on questions? The rationale for this chapter is simply that several useful comments about questions did not fit conveniently into the previous chapters.

WHAT'S THE POINT?

Since questions are not an end in themselves, let's start by looking at the possible purposes of posing questions. By and large we think of using questions as a way to get information, ideas, or opinions. Actually, questions are more often used for somewhat different purposes. Can you think of at least two other purposes for using questions? Just jot down your answers below:

Other purposes for using questions are:

1. _____
2. _____

The chances are you did not find it too difficult to come up with several other purposes for questioning. The following is a list of some of the most common uses for questions mentioned by other people who responded to the previous question about questions.

Other Purposes for Questions

1. to get the other person talking, to start up conversation
2. to guide conversation toward the topic you want to discuss, to control the conversation and keep it in the channels you desire
3. to test or evaluate the other person's knowledge or ability, an informal version of the school-exam approach
4. to show superiority, for example, by asking questions to which you know the answers and the other person does not
5. to embarrass or intimidate the other person by asking questions you are pretty sure he can't answer
6. to put off a decision by asking for more detail, more data, more alternatives, and so on, which will take time to develop

There are, however, several additional uses for questions that most people don't mention:

- questions as a way to encourage reflection or thought
- questions as an indirect way of making statements

Because we are less aware of these uses for questions, we sometimes miss a good opportunity to use a question; and sometimes we create confusion or even irritation by using a question for a purpose of which we are not fully aware.

Questioning Encourages Reflection or Thought

When you answered the question above, perhaps you came up with a use for questions that was mentioned in the list, or perhaps you came up with some other purpose. In any case, you probably did stop for a brief moment to think about the other purposes for using questions. In other words, the question encouraged you to *reflect or think about the topic of the question.* Jesse Nirenberg puts it this way in his book *Getting Through to People:*

> Since a question is a request for information, in order to supply it the other person has to move from the passive, listening state to the active, thinking one. He has to reach in his mind for the answer or perhaps work it out. Then he has to put it into language in order to communicate it.

One extremely important occasion for encouraging the other person to reflect on what you are saying is *when you want that other person to agree with you or to accept what you say and perhaps act on it.* Just because the other person nods his head or says "fine" doesn't mean he really has accepted what you say. Even if the other person paraphrases back to you what you have said, that is no guarantee that he agrees with you.

For another person truly to accept what you say, he has to "buy into it," or as the psychologists like to say, he must *own* (make his own) your thought. A question is one good way to bring about this owning process. For example, suppose you have just explained an idea or made a suggestion or given a criticism or issued an order. Here is the kind of question you might follow up with:

"Were you aware of that?"

"What do you think we should do?"

"Do you feel the same way on this?"

"Does that make sense?"

"How does that feel to you?"

There is no guarantee that asking such a question will lead the

other person to agreement or acceptance. But it will help. And
without such a question, you certainly lower your odds not only
of getting acceptance but also of *knowing* whether or not you got
it. Again, Jesse Nirenberg's book puts it nicely:

> When you are trying to influence someone's thinking,
> your responsibility does not end with putting your
> ideas into words. . . . If your communicating goes only
> as far as verbalizing your ideas, you'll not be getting
> through. . . . In order to absorb your ideas the listener
> has to mentally react to them; and you have to ask him
> to react.

Questions as an Indirect Way of Making Statements

Harold says to his friend Fred, "Would you like to go to the
movies tonight?"—a seemingly innocent-enough question serving the usual purpose of getting an opinion from someone else.
Most likely, however, there is a statement hidden behind this
question. After all, Harold didn't just mention movies at random.
He could have asked about watching TV, going to a concert,
getting some ice cream, or playing bridge. The chances are that,
in fact, *Harold* wants to go to the movies. Rather than saying this,
Harold asks Fred whether *Fred* wants to go to the movies. In such
a case Harold has somewhat exposed his position, but not really.
That is, Harold hasn't committed himself by saying what he
wants.

The theory behind this approach is that if Fred does want
to go to the movies, then everything is fine. And if Fred
doesn't want to go to the movies but would rather play cards,
then Harold can easily agree to play cards or not as he sees
fit. In essence, then, it would seem that Harold has preserved
his options, that is, he gets a "free" look at Fred's position before stating his own. Harold can thus avoid the risk of feeling
rejected because Fred doesn't accept his idea of going to the
movies; and Harold avoids the necessity of having to "give
in" to Fred's desire to play cards, because Harold never said
he wanted to do anything else (and never said he didn't want
to play cards).

Well, that's the theory; not that Harold goes through such a clear mental calculation in order to decide he will ask a question rather than state his position. Normally, the question gambit just feels safer, and Harold probably does not explicitly realize he is hiding a statement behind his question. It is precisely this lack of awareness that causes the theory to work out rather less success-fully in practice.

You see, the other person instinctively smells that something is afoot (if you'll pardon the odoriferous metaphor) behind the question. For instance, Fred may naturally wonder, why movies? or why me? Yet Fred can't be completely sure of what Harold is driving at. Perhaps Harold really doesn't care what the activity for the night is and just wants to spend some time with Fred or just wants to find out what Fred wants so that he can please (or displease) him. Or perhaps Harold doesn't want to go to the movies but thinks that Fred does and is just starting a kind of countercampaign.

So now Fred is on the spot. If he doesn't want to go to the movies, then he risks disappointing Harold. And if Fred does want to go to the movies, he still isn't sure that Harold does. One way out of the dilemma is for Fred to hedge his bets as well. Thus, Fred might reply with a vague statement or another question, and the dialogue can begin to mimic that famous scene in the Ernest Borgnine film *Marty:*

"What do you want to do, Marty?"
"I don't know, what do you want to do?"
"Oh, I don't know, what do *you* want to do?"

On the other hand, if Fred does state what he wants without hedging, then he may run into a different set of problems. For instance, suppose Fred says he would rather play cards. Then Fred may find himself in an argument when Harold indicates he really wants to go to the movies. In this scenario, Fred is likely to feel he was trapped, and the stage is set for resentment and hostility to come front and center.

Passing the Buck*

There are people who tend
To make a suggestion
By always putting it
In the form of a question.
"Shouldn't you send. . ?", they ask;
Or: "Isn't it best to sort—?"
And suddenly you find
The ball is in your court.
But I have never liked
To be pushed to the brink,
So I always come back with:
"Well, what do you think?"

—ARNOLD J. ZARETT

To help you become a bit more aware of the way statements can lurk behind a question, see if you can identify a possible statement (or want) that could underlie each of the following questions:

1. "When are you coming to bed, dear?"
   Hidden statement _____
2. "Do you love me?"
   Hidden statement _____
3. "Are you having a problem with this assignment?"
   Hidden statement _____
4. "Do you agree with Joe on this sales problem?"
   Hidden statement _____
5. "Aren't you interested in doing this?"
   Hidden statement _____
6. "When will you have the report finished?"
   Hidden statement _____
7. "Why did you spill that drink?"
   Hidden statement _____
8. "How much did you pay for that?"

*Reprinted with permission of *The Wall Street Journal.*

Hidden statement _____

9. "What are you doing tomorrow afternoon?"
   Hidden statement _____

All right, you probably found some of the hidden statements fairly easy to supply—which only shows that a lot of the time the other person is very likely to sense a statement behind this kind of question (although she may not know what to do about it). On the other hand, for some of the questions you may have had to stop and think for a bit to find a hidden statement—which only emphasizes the difficulty another person may have in determining what (or whether a) statement lies behind one of your questions.

Following are some sample hidden statements provided for each of the nine questions above. The statements you provided may differ only slightly in the wording, or they may reflect substantially different content—which only demonstrates the tricky character of hiding statements behind questions.

Sample Hidden Statements

1. "When are you coming to bed, dear?"
   Hidden statement: I'm tired, and I'd like to get to sleep soon.
2. "Do you love me?"
   Hidden statement: I wish you'd pay more attention to me.
   Another possibility: I'd like to know how I stand with you.
3. "Are you having a problem with this assignment?"
   Hidden statement: It seems to me you're having a problem.
4. "Do you agree with Joe on this sales problem?"
   Hidden statement: I think Joe is right on target.
5. "Aren't you interested in doing this?"
   Hidden statement: I don't think you're very interested.
6. "When will you have the report finished?"
   Hidden statement: I need that report by Friday.
7. "Why did you spill that drink?"
   Hidden statement: I'm really angry that you spilled that drink.

8. "How much did you pay for that?"
   Hidden statement: I hope some money is left in our budget for the rest of the month.
9. "What are you doing tomorrow afternoon?"
   Hidden statement: There's something I'd like you to do for me tomorrow afternoon.

Do you see now how many common situations involve questions that hide statements? As you become more explicitly aware of questions that cover up statements, you will probably find that a good many of your questions do fall into this category. After all, you usually have some kind of feeling or desire or position on most topics about which you converse. So it is natural that your questions on these same topics are somehow related to your wishes and opinions.

What happens is that if you know what lies behind your question, you may feel that the other person ought to know as well and respond accordingly. So you can get upset if the other person doesn't respond appropriately. Even if you don't realize you are hiding a statement behind your question, you may still be upset by a response from the other person that was not the one you desired. In either case, the other person can get upset because he is being made to guess at what lies behind your question.

You see, questions are typically used to get something for some purpose. And usually the something is for a purpose that *benefits the asker* of the question. Go back and look at the list of purposes for questions given on page 176. You will see that most of those purposes serve the asker, not the answerer, of the question. The answers to questions are used to trap, test, control, convince, or put down the person providing the answers. So another person naturally tends to be suspicious at best and at worst resentful about answering a question, at least until he knows *what* is being got at and for what purpose. Is it any wonder, then, that confusion and sometimes outright hostility can result from asking questions that mask statements or wishes?

Does all this mean you should never ask a question that masks a statement? Not at all. At times you may want to hide your true position, but you should be aware of what you are doing and realize that hiding your position may be affecting the response you get. Often, however, you will be better off at least explaining why you are asking the question:

"The reason I ask is . . .".

"I'd like to know this because . . ."

Curiosity is generally not a good reason to present. "I'm just curious" is often heard as "I have a very good reason, but I'm not willing to tell you what it is."

You may also want to consider going further and actually *express your position or desire first and then ask the question.* For instance, take any one of the sample hidden statements given previously; make that hidden statement explicit first and then follow it with the question shown, for example, "I'm tired, and I'd like to get to sleep soon. When are you coming to bed, dear?" (By the way, you should notice that all the sample hidden statements are "I" statements quite similar in format to the "I" statements discussed in chapter 7.)

But why should you expose yourself by stating your position before the other person? Well, sometimes you probably shouldn't. In many situations, however, there really is little risk in stating your position up front, and you will find out more clearly how the other person really reacts to your position. Often it is just habit that leads you to ask the question without first making the statement. So try making the statement with or without the subsequent question and see if you don't avoid a lot of needless hassle.

Now that you are more explicitly aware of questions that cover up statements, you will find that not only many of your questions fall into this category but also many questions asked of you by others. What can you do when you are on the receiving end of a question that you believe hides a statement? Well, you have several options to choose from:

1. You can take a guess at the hidden statement and respond to *it* rather than the question. For instance, when Harold asks Fred, "Would you like to go to the movies tonight?"

Fred can respond with something like, "It sounds as if you want to go to the movies. Do you?" This puts the onus back on Harold and encourages Harold to state his position.

2. Ask for more information. For instance, Fred can respond to Harold's query by saying, "I don't know, what's playing around," In a more complicated situation (say, a business discussion) you might want to ask for a review of the facts. For instance, question #4 on page 180 asks, "Do you agree with Joe on this sales problem?" You could respond by saying, "I'm not sure. Could we go over the key facts again to make sure I understand the problem?"

3. Ask for other alternatives. For instance, Fred can respond to Harold by saying, "I hadn't given it much thought. What else could we do?"

4. Say something like this: "I'd appreciate your humoring me and telling me the answer you would like [or prefer]."

YOU WANT TO AVOID LEADING QUESTIONS, DON'T YOU?

A special form of hiding a statement with a question is the so-called leading question—a question which pretty clearly indicates the desired answer right in the formulation of the question itself. For instance, consider this question: "You don't want to leave right away, do you?" The desired answer is pretty clearly, "No, I'll wait a little while." Clearly the statement behind the question is that the person asking it does not wish to leave right away. In a leading question, the statement is not very well hidden, because if it were, the questioner wouldn't be that sure of getting the desired response. Since the statement is not truly hidden, a leading question avoids confusion. But the "leading" nature of the question can still cause resentment, because the other person feels he is being told what to say and is not being allowed to make up his own mind.

Artful use of leading questions can sometimes lead the other person down your primrose path. For instance, in a lecture or speech, limited use of leading questions (or rhetorical questions, as they are sometimes called) can provide emphasis or variety and interest. Since a lecture or speech is essentially a one-way form of communication, the listener may not resent being led quite as much. In the more usual two-way conversation, a leading question is likely to raise the other person's resistance to your position. At best, a leading question does not encourage the other person to "own" what you are saying, and any acquiescence you get tends to be mere superficial politeness.

IF YOU DON'T NEED THE ANSWER, WHY ASK THE QUESTION?

Here is another kind of situation where a question masks a statement, and this time the questioner knows very well what he is doing, that is, what statement lies behind the question. For example, suppose it is absolutely vital that one of your subordinate take on a particular assignment. You proceed to ask the subordinate whether or not he would like to do the job. But you really won't take no for an answer. Like "the Godfather," you are making an offer your subordinate can't refuse. The same kind of thing can happen when you have already made a decision about something and then ask your subordinate (or your child or your spouse) what decision you ought to make. You may feel you are being tactful or indulging in so-called "participative management," but the subordinate (or the child or the spouse) will sense that he is being trapped and probably won't like it. You didn't need to ask the question, because *only one answer was acceptable* to you.

A similar kind of problem occurs when you ask a question to which *you already know the answer.* At best the question becomes a kind of test and at worst a way to embarrass or intimidate the other person. Some teachers in school resort to this technique frequently, and so do some parents in "teaching" their children and some bosses in "teaching" their subordinates.

Occasionally you may quite legitimately ask a question to which you already have the answer in order to *verify* your answer. In such situations, however, you should probably explain to the other person what you are doing. Without such an explanation, the other person will still feel that he is being asked to indulge in a guessing game, trying to guess at what you already know.

By way of summary, here is a table of the different characteristics for the several varieties of question that can mask a statement or a wish.

Summary Table

Three Types of Question Behind Which Lie Statements

Knowledge of the Statement behind
the Question by

	Question Asker	*Other Person*	*Likely Reaction*
Type I	not clearly known	not clearly known	Disagreement about the hidden statement can cause further confusion because neither person is fully aware of what the disagreement is about.
Type II leading	clearly known	clearly known	Resentment by the other person at being indirectly led.
Type III answer not needed, only one answer acceptable, or answer already known	clearly known	not clearly known	Other person can feel trapped at having responded when no response was needed or wanted; or else other person can resent being forced to play the game of guessing at what the questioner already knows.

HOW DO OPEN-ENDED AND CLOSED QUESTIONS WORK?

What you get in response to asking a question depends very much on where the question falls along these two important dimensions:

- more general to more specific
- more open-ended to more closed

The sample set of examples that follows on page 188 should help to clarify the nature of these two dimensions.

The nature of specificity and how to get it were covered in chapter 2. The general-specific dimension is raised again here because at first blush it sounds very much like the open-closed dimension, that is, a more closed question would seem to be more specific as well. But here is.the way to distinguish clearly between the two dimensions: The general-specific scale relates to the breadth with which the *topic* of the question is defined. For example, "sex" is a more general topic than "making love on an empty stomach." The open-closed scale relates more to the breadth of *response* suggested (or allowed) by the question. For example, "How do you feel about sex?" encourages a wider range of answers than "Do you like sex?"

Thus, a question can be more specific and still be phrased in a fairly open-ended way, for example, "How do you feel about making love on an empty stomach?" In that question, the topic is more specific than just "sex" in general, yet the answers could exhibit a considerable degree of variety. For example:

- "It all depends on whose stomach is empty."
- "It sounds a bit far out."
- "I'm not sure I have thought much about it."

An open-ended question is rather like an essay question on a school exam—your answer is supposed to be relevant to the question, but you can respond in any way you see fit. This is why open-ended questions are sometimes called nondirective ques-

---

Sample Set of Questions

	More Open-Ended	*More Closed*
More General	"How do you feel about sex?"	"Do you like sex?"
	"What's your opinion about sex?"	
More Specific	"How do you feel about making love on an empty stomach?"	"Would you make love on an empty stomach?"

---

tions. A closed question is more like a multiple-choice question, which directs you to a specific and limited set of possible answers. For this reason closed questions are sometimes called directive questions. Closed questions tend to encourage answers like this:

- yes, no, or maybe
- true or false
- right or wrong
- agree or disagree
- this alternative or that one

The most directive or closed question of all is the leading type of question discussed previously. A leading question doesn't even provide a choice among a few answers; it directs you to *the* answer or response.

HOW TO OPEN YOUR QUESTIONS

Generally most of us need little guidance in asking closed questions. More of our questions are closed than open, if only because so often we have a statement prowling around behind the question. So here is a handful of phrases that can help make your questions more open-ended:

"What about the . . . ?"

"Would you tell me about . . . ?"

"What is your opinion on . . . ?"

"How would you like to handle . . . ?"

"What is it that . . . ?"

"Is there anything else we should cover?"

You will find another set of open-ended phrases listed on page 13 in chapter 1, where they appear as part of the technique for getting the other person to say more.

THE DIFFERENCE IN WHAT YOU GET

There are times when you want to make a decision promptly; you want the other person to make a clear choice; you don't want to consider new options; you don't want the other person to ramble off on some related topic. In such cases you probably want your question to be more closed than open, for example, "Are we going to the movies or not?" In a legal trial, many of the questions posed by the lawyers are tightly closed, for example, "Did you or did you not . . . ?" Another example of a situation in which closed questions can be very effective is certain parts of the selling cycle. For example:

More Open-Ended	*More Closed*
"When can I make an appointment to see you?"	"Can I see you next Tuesday?"
	"Which would be more convenient for you to see me—Monday or Tuesday?"
"Are you interested in buying our product?"	"Do you prefer our deluxe model or the standard?"

On the other hand, there are times when you may want to get a fresh point of view, to consider new alternatives, to find out what is on the other person's mind (without injecting your bias), to draw out the other person's feelings. In such situations you are probably better off with the more open-ended type of question. For example, personnel interviewers find open-ended questions very useful. They know that the job applicant wants to make a good impression and will often try to say what he thinks is wanted by the interviewer. If the interviewer uses a more closed question, he risks tipping off the kind of answer he is looking for. Therefore, the interviewer asks, "What were your outside activities at school?" rather than asking "Did you participate in sports at all while you were in school?" Another example would be certain kinds of market research where it is important to avoid a biased answer or to avoid forcing the customer to respond in categories that were not really in his head. So this kind of researcher might ask, "What do you think of Schmatz pickles?" rather than asking "Do you think Schmatz pickles are good value for the money?"

In short, you stay much more in control with a closed question; you know better what kind of an answer you will get; and you may even be able to push the other person into the specific response you desire. You are less in control with an open-ended question because the response may move things in a new or different direction. But you may also find out more clearly what the other person is really thinking.

DO ALL QUESTIONS HAVE ANSWERS?

According to song lyricist Sammy Cahn, "Love and marriage go together like a horse and carriage." But our perceptions have changed since he wrote these words. Nowadays, love and marriage don't necessarily go together like a horse and carriage. And what about questions and answers? Do they always go together like a horse and carriage or only sometimes, like love and marriage?

We often assume that if a question is asked, it must have an answer. Well, language is a funny thing. Just because words make a sentence doesn't mean the sentence makes sense. And just because some words form a question doesn't mean the question has an answer. To take an extreme example, what is the answer to this question?

"What color eyes does the moon have?"

The question doesn't make any sense, you say. Exactly! But there are questions that are much less obviously nonsense, that sound perfectly reasonable, and yet these questions may not have clear answers or have possibly no answers at all. The table below provides examples of some common types of relatively unanswerable questions. The italicized words indicate the key part of the question that makes an answer difficult to find. The comments to the right of the examples briefly explain the source of difficulty in getting answers to each type of question.

Common Types of Unanswerable Questions

"*Why* does nobody like me?" "What *causes* distrust?"	"Whys" imply "becauses," and ultimate causes are often impossible to pin down.
"Is it *right* (or wrong) to make a lot of money?" "Is it *true* that a fool and his money are soon parted?" "*Should* I put my aging father in a nursing home?"	Matters of "truth," "right," and morality ("shoulds") sound absolute or objective but are generally matters of personal values and judgment.
"*Am I* a failure?" "What *is* sin?"	"Is" questions imply that the answers must involve truth and rightness—which makes answers difficult to come by. Moreover, few things are just *one* thing, for example, "I" am many things; "sin" is many things.

"What is the solution to the world energy problem?" "How can we stop countries from fighting each other?"	Some questions are just too large or too complex to have an answer or even several answers. Some problems can only be traded for other problems. The only answer to some problems is learning to live with them.
"What does this word *mean?*" "What does this painting (or poem) *mean?*"	Things don't mean anything. People give things (words and paintings and sunrises) meaning. Better to ask, "What do *you* mean?" "What does this painting (or poem) mean *to you?*"

You know children are growing up when they start asking questions that have answers.

—JOHN J. PLOMP

Now, there's nothing wrong with asking an unanswerable question every now and then. Sometimes such questions can be very thought-provoking. *The trouble comes if you don't realize that the question may be unanswerable.* The other person finds he doesn't know the answer and can't seem to figure one out. So he feels dumb or stupid. He gets frustrated or confused or angry, and so do you. The more you insist on an answer, the worse the situation gets. Or else the other person invents some answer out of desperation —an answer that usually only serves further to confuse or anger the both of you.

Scientists encounter this situation all the time, because in one sense the business of a scientist is to pose questions to nature. Their oft-quoted advice is simply this, "If you have trouble getting the answer to a question, perhaps you are asking the wrong question!"

If someone pushes you to respond to some form of unanswerable question, you can try to explain the difficulty of answering certain questions; or you can always reply with this unanswerable question of your own: "Why are you asking me this question?"

Any questions?

> *The important thing is not to stop questioning.*
>
> —ALBERT EINSTEIN

10 In Other Words

> The limits of my language mean the limits of my world.
>
> —LUDWIG WITTGENSTEIN

Well, there you have it—a vast buffet of verbal possibilities; over eighty techniques plus several alternative sets of words for some of the techniques. By way of summary, let's look at the various verbal suggestions in terms of three categories—categories that represent different dimensions of a verbal repertoire:

1. styles
2. phrasings
3. individual key words

The following comments on the categories will not provide an exhaustive relisting of all the verbal techniques in the book; but they will afford a review of many of the key approaches in a context somewhat different from that of the previous individual chapters.

Say It with Style

Style can be thought of in terms of a series of spectrums. Each spectrum has two end points or extremes. What you say is rarely a pure case of one extreme or the other. Rather, what you say typically falls somewhere *along* the spectrum *toward* one extreme

194

or the other. Several important stylistic spectrums discussed in the previous chapters are listed below, along with a few explanatory comments:

rational _____ emotional
logical   nonlogical

At the rational extreme, the conversation emphasizes consistency, logical proofs, deductive reasoning, chains of cause and effect. At the emotional extreme, feelings hold sway. The conversation is not illogical but nonlogical; logical justifications are not necessary; analytical proofs are not required.

objective ——————————————— personal

The objective style dwells on truth, correctness, rightness as established by some external higher authority; "facts" are fundamental. The personal end of the spectrum emphasizes the subjective nature of experience; "facts" and the truth are considered highly relative. Most of what we say, then, becomes no more and no less than opinion. In the personal style, the validity of what we say comes from the fact that *we* say it, and on those grounds alone it must be reckoned with.

general ————————————— specific

A general style avoids the clutter of a myriad of details. Generalities abstract the common elements from all the detail and thus simplify what might otherwise be an unmanageably complex situation. Talking in general terms can be both convenient and very powerful. On the other hand, getting specific pins down the detail of what we really mean, what exactly is involved, how it might be applied. The difference between general and specific is the difference between the aerial photo of a city and the ground view.

loose _____ tight
approximative   literal

The loose end of this spectrum of style was not discussed at great length in any of the chapters of this book. In brief, the loose style can involve inexact metaphors, ambiguities, and half-apt ideas. And this imprecise style can be very useful, for example, for stimulating creativity, maintaining group cohesion, grappling with the unknown. For other purposes, though, it can be important to move toward the other end of the spectrum, which pins things down more exactly and thoroughly. Note that there is a difference between this stylistic spectrum and the general-specific spectrum. A generality can be very succinct, clear, and comprehensive, or it can be rather loose and fuzzy.

problem solving _____ argumentative
                                                  opinion-oriented

The problem-solving style emphasizes working jointly on a task. Objections, criticism, and disagreement become ways of working on the problem. The goal is the solution or action. At the other end of the spectrum, the accent is on winning the argument, getting the other person to change her opinion (which, of course, is one way of solving a problem). Objections, criticism, and rebuttals are ways of scoring the battle. The goal is to run up the point total.

Where you fall on each of these stylistic spectrums is not good or bad in any absolute sense. Rather, where you fall is merely more appropriate or less appropriate to a particular situation and the kind of conversation you want to have. Move along any one of the spectrums away from one extreme toward the other and the nature of the conversation will change, different information will emerge, different attitudes will come into play.

If you are aware of these stylistic spectrums, you can explicitly state what style of conversation you would like to have, for example, "I'd like to get more specific now" or "Could we look at this thing from an emotional, not necessarily a logical, point of view for a minute?" Awareness of the style spectrums also allows you to realize that the other person may not be talking from the same place on a spectrum as you are. For instance, you may be trying to go at something in a very loose, approximative way, whereas the other person may be trying to carry on a very tight, literal discussion. The resulting conversation can be very confusing or frustrating for both of you. Once you notice a stylistic discrepancy between you and the other person, then you are in a much better position to do something about it, that is, modify your style or try to get the other person to modify his.

Turning a Phrase

One way to characterize phrases is to place them in such categories as wish, belief, need, information, command, request, and so on. The principle behind some of the techniques in this book is to change the character of a phrase from one of these categories to another:

- phrasing an objection as a wish, for example, "That's too expensive" becomes "I wish it weren't so expensive."
- phrasing a criticism as a problem to be solved, for example, "That idea won't work because it will take too much time" becomes *"The problem* in your idea *is how to* get it to take less time."
- phrasing a need (or moral obligation) as a wish, for example, "I really need a vacation" becomes "I'd really like to take a vacation."
- phrasing a question as a statement, for example, "Do you want to go to the movies tonight?" becomes "I'd like to go to the movies tonight."

Such changes in phrasing leave the content of what you say pretty much the same, but the tone, the mood, the positioning of what you say can shift dramatically—with significant impact on the subsequent conversation.

Some of the other techniques that involved phrasing were of a different nature. These techniques did not involve changing a phrase from one category to another. Rather they suggested the uses of new (or less common) categories of phrasing. For example:

- elicitive phrases—a category of phrases that lead the other person to say some more, to elaborate or expand, for example, "Tell me some more"; "Could you expand on that?"
- paraphrase—feeding back the verbal or nonverbal parts of what you hear and see to clarify what is going on, to prove you are listening, to test your understanding, for example, "It sounds as if you're saying. . . . Is that it?" "So if I understand you. . . . Right?"
- public writing—a particular use of paraphrase that involves writing down the paraphrase in full view to facilitate understanding and reduce rambling and to encourage building on ideas.
- repetition—to make clear that you really mean what you are saying.
- open-ended questions—allowing the other person a wider choice of how to respond in order to encourage a fresh point of view or to find out what is on the other person's mind without injecting your bias, for example, "Would you tell me about . . . ?" "What is your opinion on . . . ?"

You will notice that these categories of phrasing are somehow different from the previous categories of a wish, belief, need, and so on. These categories are what might be called process categories—their primary function is to affect the way the conversation is flowing, without necessarily presenting any particular idea, thought, or opinion.

What a Difference a Word Makes

One word can change the whole feel of what you say and how the other person responds. One word can open up more choices, encourage expression of feelings, pin down a detail, indicate tolerance for another viewpoint. What follows is an alphabetical listing of most of the key individual words discussed in the previous chapters. Beside each word is a brief comment on what the word can do.

Key Word(s)	Comments on How the Word(s) Work(s)
"always"	rarely accurate; not very specific; tends to antagonize the other person
"and" (instead of "but")	helps encourage more than one point of view; avoids either-or attitude
"are"	implies factual quality or eternal truth; creates either-or framework; provides no escape hatch unless qualified
"because"	leads to rational, logical explanation in terms of cause and effect
"but"	often an "eraser" of what was said previously; emphasizes one aspect of something to the near exclusion of other aspects
"can't"	implies no choice, that is, "forced to"; usually requires providing reasons or explanation
"constantly"	rarely accurate; not very specific; tends to antagonize the other person
"could be"	conditional term; provides escape hatch
"everything"	rarely accurate; not very specific; tends to antagonize the other person
"every time"	rarely accurate; not very specific; tends to antagonize the other person
"have to"	implies no choice, that is, claims a basic "need" is involved; often a wish in disguise

"how"	leads to discussion of something's *structure* rather than its *cause* (or the "why"); can provide more specifics than "What?"
"how come"	a form of "Why?" leading to rational, logical explanation in terms of cause and effect
"how many"; "how much"; "how often"	leads to quantification and the high level of specificity conveyed by numbers
"I" (instead of "you," "he," "it," or "they")	helps establish the subjective, personal nature of what is said; forces speaker to take responsibility for what he says
"interesting"	good "cop-out" word; sounds positive but doesn't commit to a position
"is"	implies factual quality or eternal truth; creates either-or framework; provides no escape hatch unless qualified
"maybe"	conditional term; provides escape hatch
"must"	implies no choice, that is, claims a basic "need" is involved; often a wish in disguise
"need to"	implies no choice; often a wish in disguise
"never"	rarely accurate; not very specific; tends to antagonize the other person
"new"	key word in asking for eye-opening advice
"now" (as in "right now")	helps clarify that a comment or a "no" applies to a particular, present situation or condition for the moment

"ought to"	implies no choice, that is, claims speaker is forced by the imposition of an external code; often a wish in disguise
"perhaps"	conditional term; provides escape hatch
"possibly"	conditional term; provides escape hatch
"should"	implies no choice, that is, claims speaker is forced by the imposition of an external code; often a wish in disguise
"sometimes"	conditional term; provides escape hatch
"so what"	implies irrelevance; pushes for more detail; often taken as a put-down; better asked with a phrasing such as "What is the effect of that on . . . ?"
"want to"	implies personal choice or desire; most likely what a "need" or a "should" really is
"what"	probes for description; a good first question for getting specifics
"what if"	probes for relationships between the elements in a situation or problem; teases out more detail
"when"	really pins things down
"where"	really pins things down
"wish to"	implies personal choice or desire; more likely what a "need" or a "should" really is
"who"	a key question where action is involved; nothing gets done unless you know who will do it; "the how is who"

"why"	leads to rational, logical explanation in terms of cause and effect; moves talk away from feelings; may be a bad first question
"won't" or "don't want to" (instead of "can't")	implies personal choice; reasons not necessarily required

TALK WITH A DIFFERENCE

Are there other verbal formulas not covered in this book? Of course! You probably have a few special ones of your own that weren't covered. And you're likely to invent a few more new ones after reading this book. Are the verbal techniques presented in the previous chapters just a random collection of generally useful tricks of the trade? Not really. The particular verbal alternatives suggested in this book spring from a rather special set of interrelated philosophical premises—call them values or personal observations of the world and the people in it.

1. *Reality is complex.* Complexity means not only the large number of bits and pieces that exist but also the sizable number of interrelationships that tie together the bits and pieces. This complexity means that in most situations, we really cannot talk about everything. We inevitably end up discussing only pieces and parts, selected relationships within the whole. Often we end up talking about different pieces from those the other person is talking about.
2. *Reality is highly subjective.* Most of what we experience is very personal. What we see and hear is rarely the same as what the other person is seeing and hearing.
3. *There are many versions of reality.* Because reality is complex and because we project our own biases upon and select from that reality, there are many versions of reality. To decide once and for all whether something is really x rather than y may be an impossible task. It is more likely that the something is both x and y (and a number of other things as well).

4. *Ideas, thoughts, and words tend to be approximations.* As individuals (and as a species) we are constantly evolving, always changing. No one has the definitive answer to anything. Even our internal visions are rarely complete and fully detailed. And the translations of those internal feelings or pictures into words always lose something in the process. What gets said is never the whole thing, even if it sounds as if it is.

5. *Understanding is usually suspect.* Because reality is complex and subjective and because ideas are approximations, true understanding is difficult (even unlikely). Understanding someone else (and even ourselves) does not come easy. The odds are that most of the time we don't fully understand the other person (and vice versa).

6. *Personalities are fragile.* Most of us do feel "not okay" most of the time; and that's not likely to change no matter which books we read, what religion we adopt, or which psychiatrist we consult. Our conversation needs to take account of this fragility; our conversation needs to sustain the integrity of the other person's person.

These six premises are not terribly exotic, but they do go against the spirit of the popular mythology that continually bombards us. Many books, TV shows, advertisements, along with a lot of cocktail chatter, lead us to believe that reality can be made simple if we are just clever enough to figure out how to do it; that we all share a common sense of reality if we can just overcome our personal prejudices; that people can communicate clearly and fully to each other if only they pay a little attention to what they are saying.

It is not surprising that the normal patterns of talking often reflect the premises of the popular mythology. Since the verbal approaches of this book are based on a rather different set of premises, they offer significantly different alternatives. That is why the verbal formulas in this book tend to generate results and reactions quite different from those of the more common verbal gambits. Of course, you can still use these alternative verbal formulas even if you don't subscribe fully to the special set of premises behind them. As long as the techniques produce useful results for you, that is all that really counts.

Unfortunately, no matter how intrigued you may be by the verbal techniques in this book, they won't do anything for you unless you use them. So before signing off, the next section summarizes the thoughts scattered in the previous chapters about how to incorporate the ideas in this book into your conversation.

TRY 'EM, YOU'LL LIKE 'EM

Changing what you say is a lot easier than making some other kinds of changes, but a change is still involved. You are probably pretty comfortable with the verbal habits you have built up over the years. Even if those habits don't always produce the kind of result you would like, at least you sort of know what to expect. There is a kind of inertia that works against your adopting the verbal alternatives presented in this book. In other words, you probably won't utilize some of the verbal alternatives in this book without making a conscious effort.

Here are some suggestions (in the form of a six-step approach) that can help you incorporate new verbal formulas into your conversation.

1. Simply become more aware of the alternatives or options for what you say. (If you have read the previous chapters, your awareness is already aroused.)
2. The next step is just to listen—listen to the conversations of others and to the conversations you have. Don't try yet to use any of the new verbal formulas you have been reading about. Just listen with your new awareness to the formulas that you and others use now. You may be surprised at how much more clearly you recognize various verbal gambits, and you will notice much more about how those gambits work or don't work for various situations.
3. Consciously select one of the verbal approaches suggested in this book. Select one that appeals to you, that seems to make sense, that doesn't appear difficult or strange for you

to try. Make it easy on yourself. For starters don't pick a new approach that strikes you as highly esoteric or very risky. And don't select more than one. You'll just clutter your head. Remember that using the verbal formulas need not be an all-or-nothing matter. Using just one or two new techniques some of the time can still put you ahead of the game.

4. Next you may want to rehearse privately the use of the verbal formulas you selected. The exercises in the previous chapters do provide some practice for some of the techniques, but it is worth doing a bit more. Of course, you can rehearse the words and situation silently in your head. It is much better, however, to do your rehearsing out loud. You might even want to do your talking to a tape recorder so that you can hear how you sound.

In your rehearsal just imagine a particular situation in which you might want to use one of your selected techniques. Then talk out *both* sides of the conversation, verbalizing what the other person might say as well as what you would say.

This rehearsal step is included because it is a step that is often overlooked. And many people feel awkward or embarrassed about talking out loud to themselves even in the privacy of an empty room. But don't view rehearsing verbal formulas out loud as a sign of senility or the manifestation of some severe psychiatric disorder. Experienced public speakers rehearse their speeches, teachers rehearse their lectures, negotiators or courtroom lawyers often role-play aloud various dialogues that they anticipate might occur.

5. Now you want to decide in what conversation you will try out your selected new verbal formulas, and this is worth thinking about. Anything new is bound to feel a bit different. You won't know exactly what you will say, how it will work into the conversation, what will happen as a result. In short, you may feel a bit uneasy. It is not that the formulas will necessarily sound strange or peculiar to the other person —usually they won't. It is just that you may feel strange trying out something new.

The best way to deal with this feeling of strangeness is by trying out the new thing in a setting that is safe, a situation that doesn't really count. It's much like a scientist who first tries an experiment in the safety and controlled conditions of a laboratory.

Of course, in life it's hard to find a perfectly safe situation. Everything counts, more or less. Just pick a situation that counts less rather than more. Pick a fairly mundane issue like where to eat lunch or how the local athletic team is doing. Moreover, don't try the techniques out on someone whom you feel it important to impress, a new boss, for example. Try out the techniques first with a good friend, someone who will continue to think well of you even if you're feeling awkward. As a matter of fact, sometimes a stranger is the perfect person on whom to try a new technique—someone you don't know and don't care about and probably won't see again.

6. Go ahead and try 'em. You don't have to make any explanation. Most of the verbal approaches in this book can be used without the other person having to know what you're trying; the techniques are not rules that both parties must accept and obey to play the game.

On the other hand, you may feel less uneasy about trying out the techniques if you do explain to the other person what you are doing. Simply say to your friend something like: "Look, I've been reading this book that has some interesting ideas about different ways to say things. And there are a couple of approaches I'd like to try out as we talk so that I can see how they work. Is that all right with you?" You can even describe (at least in general terms) the specific techniques you want to try out. Whether or not you make this kind of explanation beforehand, you might want to discuss the experiment with your friend afterward. Get his reactions; talk about how the conversation was affected; discuss how you might improve your use of the technique the next time.

The idea is for you to become comfortable with the technique; modify it and adapt it to your own personal style and needs.

After all this, you are on your own. You'll probably find the formulas easier to use than you thought. But be aware that any verbal approach can be sabotaged by your tone of voice or by other nonverbal gestures. And if you consciously choose to use the techniques in an artificial, devious fashion, the results may be quite different from those described in this book.

Does all this mean you should drop your current verbal formulas in favor of the ones recommended in this book? Absolutely not! What you have now is simply a few more options, a few more tools in your old kit bag. You have more than one way to skin a chat.

Will you use any one of the new formulas all the time? Probably not! Not every statement can or should be an "I" statement. If you paraphrase everything that someone says, you may find that person not talking very often with you. Sometimes you need a "but" instead of an "and." Unfortunately there is no good way to prescribe exactly when a particular verbal technique is appropriate and when it is not. And *you* will use the verbal formulas in different ways and for somewhat different situations than anyone else.

On the other hand, you should realize that most of the techniques are widely applicable. For instance, "I" statements can be very effective with your boss as well as your lover, with a doctor as well as a friend. All of the techniques in the book have been used productively in conversations between people in such diverse roles as these:

parent and child	client and expert (e.g., doctor, lawyer)
husband and wife	teacher and pupil
lovers	boss and subordinate
friends	salesman and customer

And all of the techniques have been used in conversations with purposes that range as broadly as these:

problem solving	griping
evaluating alternatives	negotiating
decision making	mediating disputes or quarrels
transmitting information	persuading or convincing
planning	generating and building ideas
instructing	creating feelings of closeness or involvement
appraising personnel	calming down heated discussions

In short, the techniques are much more widely applicable than you probably think! Try 'em, you'll like 'em—and so will the other person.

Suggested Readings

The books listed below represent only a small number of the many books that provided ideas and insights for the subjects treated in this volume. The books chosen for this list were those that tended to present a number of specific verbal techniques.

Alberti, Robert E., Ph.D.; and Emmons, Michael L., Ph.D. *Stand Up, Speak Out, Talk Back!: The Key to Self-Assertive Behavior.* New York: Pocket Books, 1975.

Bower, Sharon and Gordon. *Asserting Yourself: A Practical Guide for Positive Change.* Reading, Mass.: Addison Wesley, 1976.

Carnegie, Dale. *How to Win Friends and Influence People.* New York: Pocket Books, 1974 (original edition 1936).

Feldman, Sandor S., M.D. *Mannerism of Speech and Gestures in Everyday Life.* New York: International Universities Press, 1959.

Fensterhem, Herbert, Ph.D.; and Baer, Jean. *Don't Say Yes When You Want to Say No.* New York: David McKay, 1975.

Ginott, Dr. Haum G. *Between Parent and Child.* New York: Macmillan, 1965.

Hayakawa, S. I. *Language in Thought and Action,* 3rd ed. New York: Harcourt Brace Jovanovich, 1972.

Johnson, Wendell. *Your Most Enchanted Listener.* New York: Harper & Row, 1956.

Lopez, Felix M. *Personnel Interviewing: Theory and Practice.* New York: McGraw-Hill, 1975.

Maier, Norman R. F. *Problem Solving Discussions and Conferences.* New York: McGraw-Hill Book Co., 1963.

Miller, Sherod; Nunnally, Elam; and Wackman, Daniel B. *Alive and Aware: Improving Communication in Relationships.* Minneapolis: Interpersonal Communications Programs, Inc., 1975.

Nirenberg, Jesse S. *Getting Through to People.* Englewood Cliffs, N.J.: Prentice Hall, 1963.

Perls, Fritz. *The Gestalt Approach and Eye Witness to Therapy.* Palo Alto, Calif.: Science and Behavior Books, 1973.

Sax, Saville, and Hollander, Sandra. *Reality Games.* New York: Macmillan, 1972.

Smith, Gerald Walker. *Hidden Meanings.* Millbrae, Calif.: Celestial Arts, 1975.

Smith, Manuel J. *When I Say No, I Feel Guilty.* New York: Dial Press, 1975.

Index

Hidden statements
  behind questions, 178–186
  relationship to "I" statements, 183
  responding to, 183–184
"How"
  to find out "what," 34–35
  is who, 36
"How come?" (or How could that
  be?"), 35

"I," what comes after the, 145–165
Ideas
  as approximations, 82
  credit of, 84–85
  criticizing instead of person, 54
  as extension of self, 47
  as eye-opening help, 101
  not taking literally, 80–81
  uniqueness of, 29
"I feel" statements, 150–152
Impact. *See* Effect
Important. *See* Most important thing
Information, eye-opening help, 101
Insights, as eye-opening help, 101
      See also Paraphrase; Under-
      standing
Instruction, as eye-opening help, 101
Insults. *See* Criticism
"Interesting," as cop-out phrase, 106
Interpreting, versus reporting, 148–
  150
"Is" question, as unanswerable, 191
"Is" statements, 136–138
  avoiding in criticism, 52–53
  describing attributes, not personal
    reaction, 137
  escape hatches in, 53, 138–139
  impersonality of, 136
  inclusive nature of, 137
  making subjective, 139
  related verb phrases, 53
  substituting "I" statements for,
    139–144
"I" statements
  examples of, 142–143
  as good way to speak for self, 139–
    144
  hidden behind questions, 183
  in talking about feelings of others,
    156

Japanese style of decision-making,
  116–117
Judgment. *See* Opinion

Key words, list of, 199–202

Likes. *See* Credits
Limitations. *See* Conditions
Listening, suggested by repetition,
  12
      See also Paraphrase; Under-
      standing
Lists, of verbal techniques. *See* Sum-
      mary charts
Literal style, 196
Logic
  emphasis on, in schooling, 153
  in feelings, 154
  as style, 196
Logic chopping, avoidance of, in get-
      ting advice, 109
Loose style, 196

Manipulation, through verbal tech-
      niques, 4
"Maybe"
  as "definite maybe," 125
  as escape hatch, 53, 138
Meetings, paraphrase in, 22–24
Merit. *See* Credits
Metaphor
  in elaborating feelings, 153
  in loose style, 196
"Might be," as escape hatch, 53, 138
Mind asking, 156
Mind reading, avoidance of, 156
Moral support, 97–99
More. *See* asking for more
Most important thing, 8–24
"Must be"
  as expression of needs, 162
  as expression of wants, 163
  as verb phrase related to "is," 138

Needs
  acknowledgment of, before saying
    no, 122–23
  wants and, 161–163
"Never," avoidance of
  in crediting, 86
  in criticism, 60–61
"New," as key word in asking for
    help, 104
No, saying, 119–132
  acknowledgment of other's need
    or problem in, 122–123
  asking for more information be-
    fore, 122

Personal *(continued)*
  putting self back into, 134–135, 139, 154–155
  techniques of, 169–171
    summary chart of techniques for, 172–173
  visual paraphrase in, 148–150
  when to use, 168
  wishes and wants and, 160–165
    See also Feelings; Subjective; Wants; Uniqueness
Personalities. *See* Self
Phrasings, types of changes in, 197–198
Pollyanna principle, 120
Positives, pushing for, 77–82
  See also Credits
Possibility. *See* Escape hatches
"Possibly," as escape hatch, 53, 138
Praise. *See* Credits
Premises behind techniques, 202–204
Probing. *See* Specifics
Problem
  acknowledging before saying no, 122–123
  versus solution orientation in getting advice, 117
Problem-solving
  as approach to criticism, 63
  style of, 196
Process
  as bother, 55
  crediting with content, 81–82
  criticizing with content, 55–57
Proof
  of credit, 87
  of criticism, 61
  of hearing, listening, understanding, 14–20
    See also Paraphrase; Understanding
Pros (and cons). *See* Credits
Public writing, 22–24

Quantification, 31
Questions, 175–193
  closed, 187–189
  different results from open and closed, 189–190
  directive, 187–189
  examples of statements hidden behind, 180–182

Questions *(continued)*
  general, 12–13
  in getting other to say more, 12–13
  in getting specifics, 30–37
  with hidden statements, 178–186
    response to, 183–184
    summary chart of, 186
  leading, 184–185, 188
  nondirective, 12–13, 187–189
  open-ended, 12–13, 187–189
  paraphrase as a form of, 18
  purposes of, 175–178
  quantitative types of, 31
  reflection encouraged by, 177–178
  before saying no, 122
  as serving the asker, 182
  unanswerable, 190–193
  to which answers not needed, 185
  wishes hidden behind, 178–186
  without clear answers, 190–193

Rational style, 195
Reaction, stifling in getting advice, 106–108
Reality, multiple versions of, 135, 202
Reasons
  giving in saying no, 128–130
  presenting to avoid 3rd degree, 42
  standard list of, for saying no, 130
Recommendations. *See* Conclusions
Reflecting. *See* Paraphrase
Relevance, asking about as means to specifics, 37
Repetition
  asking for, 12
  to encourage expansion, 12
  of no, 130–131
Rephrasing. *See* Paraphrase
Requests and orders, 121–122
Responses
  to credits, 91–92
  to eye-opening help, 101–118
  nondirective, 13–14, 187–190
  that ask for more, 11–14
    See also Asking; Questions
Restating. *See* Paraphrase
Results. *See* Effect
Rhetorical questions, 184–185, 188
Right. *See* truth
Risk
  avoidance by question, 178–186
  in saying no, 120